Silence
& its tongues

Author's note

Robyn Rowland has written eight books, five of them poetry. Her most recent, *Shadows at the Gate,* was published in 2004 by Five Islands Press. It is set primarily in Ireland, where she has lived and worked over a 22 year period, reading and teaching at most major literary festivals there, including, Cúirt International Festival of Literature, Listowel Writers Week, Scríobh, Éigse Michael Hartnett, Boyle Arts Festival, Clifden Arts Week, The Yeats Society, and Strokestown International Poetry Festival. In Australia, her readings/panels have included Perth International Arts Festival, Adelaide Writers Week, Melbourne Writers Week, The Australian Poetry Festival, and the Tasmanian Poetry Festival. Her work has been published in Australia, Ireland, Japan, Canada, the U.S. and New Zealand.

In 2004/2005 ABC Radio National's *PoeticA* featured her work in a programme titled 'Shadows at the Gate: the poetry of Robyn Rowland', covering three of her books. ABC Radio National's *The Spirit of Things* covered her Irish experience of exile and belonging in an extended interview, 'Inspirited Landscapes'. In 2002 she won both the Catalpa Poetry Prize and the overall Writers' Prize from the Australian-Irish Heritage Association. She has been a poetry judge for the Fellowship of Australian Writers, Society of Women Writers Victoria, Australian Capital Territory Writer's Centre Poetry Prize, and W.B. Yeats Australian and New Zealand Poetry Prize.

Previously Professor of Social Inquiry at Deakin University, **Dr Robyn Rowland AO**, spent 18 years creating critiques of reproductive technology and genetic engineering, producing her book *Living Laboratories. Women and Reproductive Technology* in 1992. Her work was used by national and international committees in framing legislation, and she has addressed the House of Lords, London, on embryo experimentation. She was made an Officer in the Order of Australia for her contribution to higher education and women's health in 1996, and retired that year from academic life after breast cancer and burnout.

www.robynrowland.com

Other Books by Robyn Rowland

Poetry

Shadows at the Gate. Five Islands Press, Wollongong, 2004

Fiery Waters. Five Islands Press, Wollongong, 2001

Perverse Serenity. Heinemann, Australia, 1990. Spinifex, Australia, 1992

Filigree in Blood. Longman Cheshire, Melbourne, 1982

Other Books

Living Laboratories. Women and reproductive technology. Pan MacMillan, Australia, 1992; Lime Tree, U.K. and Canada; Indiana University Press, U.S. 1993; and Cedar Press, U.K. 1993

Woman Herself. A transdisciplinary perspective on women's identity. Oxford University Press, Melbourne, 1988

Women who do and women who don't, join the women's movement, editor, Routledge and Kegan Paul, London and New York, 1984

To Dear Brendan,

Silence
& its tongues

Robyn Rowland

*with admiration for
your work
& for your love
of poetry,
fondest
regards,*

Five Islands Press

*Clydon
Arts Week*

*Robyn
Sept 2006*

Published by Five Islands Press Pty Ltd,
School of Creative Arts, University of Melbourne
03 8344 8713
email: rpretty@unimelb.edu.au

Cover painting: 'The dream', Lynda Burke
Cover design: Kathryn Junor
Back Cover photo: Lynda Burke, Errislannan

National Library of Australia
Cataloguing-in-Publications Entry
Rowland, Robyn 1952–
Silence and its tongues
ISBN 0 7340 3648 5

1. Title.
A821.3

This project has been assisted by the Commonwealth Government
through the Literature Board of the Australia Council,
the Federal Government's arts funding and advisory body.

Acknowledgements

My deep appreciation to publisher Ron Pretty for his enduring contribution to Australian poetry.

To Lynda Burke in Ireland: thanks for your friendship, and for permission to use your lovely painting, 'The dream', on the cover.

Thanks also to poetry friends in Australia and Ireland who have assisted me by contributing valuable comments on some poems in this manuscript, particularly Barry Hill and Alex Skovron. Special thanks to Jennifer Harrison; friend, poet and 'workshop mate'.

As always, thanks to my father Norm Rowland, for his practical and loving support. To my sons Ennis and Tully, who live side-by-side with all the difficulties and, hopefully, delights of a mother-poet; my love and gratitude.

Some poems in this book explore depression, possibly inherited, definitely learned. Tracking and understanding its source; learning to manage it; and continuing to struggle towards the light, takes work. Living sometimes in what I think of, and call in this book, the Dark, does not rule out a life with warmth and joy. Thank you to those friends who, in sharing their friendship, add to the brightness of life.

Poems in this collection have been published in the following journals, sometimes with slight rewriting: *Agenda* (UK), *Island, the Australian, Arena, Space, Mindfire*, and the anthology *English at Eleven Vce Units 1&2, 2e*, (John Wiley and Sons, Queensland, 2006).

'Silence' was published in *The Best Australian Poems*, 2005, edited by Les Murray (Black Inc., Melbourne, 2005) and 'This moon' was published in *The Best Australian Poems 2006*, edited by Les Murray, (Black Inc., Melbourne, 2006). 'The strength of words' was awarded second prize in the *International Poetry Prize*, Melbourne Poets' Union, 2005; 'Blue line' was second in the *Martha Richardson Medal Poetry Competition*, 2005.

This work was assisted by the award of a *Varuna Writers' Retreat Fellowship*, 2005. Many thanks for the opportunity there for silence, and the collegial 'madness' of like-minded writers.

Contents

The path into the light seems dark,
the path forward seems to go back.

Lao-Tzu

I

Silence & its tongues

Dispatch from the dome

Inside this canopy, terrain is variable:
now a confusion of rainforest tangled in vine,
coloured birds bright in flight
absent the squabble of song;
now a desert at night, its dry road
so very long across the naked plain,
windless, without the whirr of crickets
though their translucent wings are working hard.
Whatever landscape, this vault endures,
inside shimmering walls sealing out sound.

Beyond it, sibilance of sea is drowned
in the quiescence between two waves.
A match burns quiet after its scratched flare.
Even breath pauses – still –
between the tidal swirl of in and out,
hesitating on sand,
almost stranded.
These unuttered moments are small but seminal
beside a greater silence
under this impervious dome.

Words are the only messages out.
Somehow it is their gift, their nature,
to slip between fine seams of fabric,
a topology of connection only they know.
But it's a one-way crack they slip through,
a tiny valve on a child's blow-up water-tube.
Nothing penetrates back. Perhaps they never make it,
though sometimes I see hieroglyphics
pressed in mute braille against these transparent walls,
their calligraphy the lost thread of the labyrinth.

I thought I sensed your presence in here,
it startled me like shadows,
and when you wrote, I imagined
a sensibility attuned,
rhythms of thought familiar as old songs,
a curved arm warm as a companion.
But these had gathered ethereal as utterance.
This is where I have always lived – I knew that –
receptor for a silence that cannot be broken,
aloneness that cannot be spoken.

I have tried to press my mouth
to spaces that might be opening lips.
I think of the velvet moss of giant clams
thick along their jagged smile
that lightly touched, disappears.
I think of the taste of honey,
of moon's scattered sweat along your back,
soft fur of your skin under my tongue.
I think of your voice during love, unvowelled, guttural.
I think of any voice. I long for it.

The strength of words

In Novgorod, Russians are digging up their medieval past:
chess pieces, a toy horse, a brooch, a stylus for writing.
For eighty years archaeologists and students have sifted
mud and dust on banks of the river Volkhov,
conduit for trade with Turkey and the Byzantine Empire.
Flourishing city, enlightened –
peasants, nobility, even women, wrote.
Marriage, desire, a child's writing lesson,
a landlord's politics, starvation –
everything changing and unchanged.
Letters to explain an error, to stop a brother's anger,
to commission a painting,
carefully pieced together ten centuries on.
The painter Grechin's rediscovered ownership of frescoes
still exquisite in their detail and devotion,
detected by notes; by his signature mistakes on the walls of a church.
One thousand letters written on birch bark
sending out the price of wheat or a plea for love:
'Marry me. I want you. You want me.'
Letters give up names, the names faces –
'a thousand letters, a thousand voices.'
And I still wait on one.

Silence

The blind spins up
snatched by the window frame.
I gaze at this blank day.
Here are trees so very green
against the blanched sky;
no clouds, no fog,
just the back of a mirror,
a pearl in shadow,
a marble sepulchre.
Beneath, grey fences stained with rain,
a pewter water-slick on the concrete drive.
You do not call or write.
Even to one trained for years
in the interpreting of its dialects,
silence is a cold and difficult language.

Venice
  for Aodh

Sirens thrill along mute canals near midnight.
I count the required sixteen for flood warning.
Water laps intimate under the window at Hotel *Tre Archi*
swelling across cobbled *fondamenta* beneath.
I watch from the second floor, knowing others
hoist quickly their chairs to the ceiling
elsewhere in ground floor rooms.
The sea is making inroads across islands of disbelief.
Lovers drink from each others lips
between sparse street lamps,
feet soaked in salt.

Here I am only lost walking, never on the water.
Hail came suddenly in the afternoon,
lightning jolting the boat from Murano
shattering talk and the bare uplifted faces.
I remember your eyes.
I drink wine from a jug: ruby-red, fat and round, the taste.
Your kisses still stroll across my tongue with it
though you are oceans away.
Every filigree of connection the body makes from lips
 – around a breast, along a thigh –
shiver down deep, inside fig-pink memory.

Masks are hanging from the walls
crowding windows of small shops
in the market off *Canale di Cannaregio.*
Silver and peacock-blue, raven-black and scarlet,
their shape-shifting visages await the gift of sight
we alone can position there.
Here is the place to lose myself.
One step inside this face of gold: all children left behind, all worries,
and the dent of daily life in the goblet of fancy evades recognition

along with the name, the obligation of returning.
Sheathed with disguise, it is free.
I could do anything here.

Venice is an old lover still wet with longing
her body unashamed,
everywhere bridges over a maze of aqueous veins,
the map of love's capillaries
with some dead-ends, some narrow ways,
some bridges a gondola can only pass under
if I lean heavily to one side
while the boatman dances his oar
against the wooden rollick.
You have to pay.

Venice is sinking, but slowly enough.
Gates can be erected to block the hungry tide that
surges, purling courtship between water and stone.
Sea comes for me tonight.
Maybe it carries our breath from the lake near your door;
rain off our shoulders in Fahy's Wood at *Bealtaine*;
dew from your purple tulips and uncut meadowsweet.
Images of you clutter my mind's alleyways,
slip like shadows between corner and canal.
They rouse longing in a city of water and glass,
liquid cold, fluid hot.

Caravaggio-dark, skies were sanguineous at sunset.
Now mist inside shutters
shrouds the Venetian glitter of light splayed on walls
from red and blue buds
in the Murano chandelier.
Tonight is full moon.
A mist of rain rings her wide-eyed light,
loneliness
a single beam down the smudged waterway.

If only this small light
or this dark night
or the sea's impatient working
at the foundations of this old wall,
could prise ajar the future
momentarily –
and you are there on a shore somewhere,
waiting.
This is a city of indulgence, and
I'd pay the boatman twice,
if he'd bring you.

– *Fahy's Wood* is pronounced *Fah- hee's* in Irish.
– *Bealtaine:* (pron, *bal*-tin-uh) old Celtic festival on May Day, the coming of summer and the light.

Walking away
for Aodh

Outside Hanley's pub that wet May Irish day,
I found on tin-gray pavement in a storm,
a tulip bud, cut abrupt.
Plum purple, it satin-slipped inside my palm.

Sensing brevity of time – seven hours perhaps –
its yellow starfish-heart opened to my body's heat
lusting for sunlight it could not find in that dark bar,
where only fiddle flashed out sweet rods of light
to challenge nailing rain.
I held it out for you, this bud,
to show you how like your own fine tulip blooms it was,
sliding sinuous in your garden,
leaning against primroses, and into golden daisies for warmth.

Your fence was barely there to guard your house –
so low, more fairy ring than fort.
My fence at home is high and rough.
Ti-tree sheds more bark each year,
it shields me from storms, intruders, florid love.
Yet that fence was a world away – and fifteen days.

I remember
there were diamond skies blistering with stars,
bubble of moon almost full,
and a fat slice of light
where fabric of blood-black night had split,
to show us curled to each other,
intimate as strangers can be
in a hurry.

There was your mastery I admired,
to be so free of family cares.
There was Sinéad singing and your eyes bird-egg blue
worshipping the ground on which she walks,
and nothing, so far, 'compares to you'.
There were books on bedroom shelves
jangling together to trace the angled map of your mind –
economics, history, Yeats, Joyce –
and Campbell inciting me to follow my 'bliss'.
But I can't follow it there
for all your ancient songs in those short days.

Detail imprints in my skin
makes it hard for me to walk away, forget,
erase the ease of your quick laugh,
your soft mouth inside my wrist.
Something dangerous you gave me
I never knew was sharp.
Solicitude left its phantom ache;
the softest etching in a scrimshaw scar.

– Sinéad: Irish singer Sinéad O'Connor

Cherry dust

for Aodh

Around me tangled sheets like softened fields,
above, your eyes, bluebells, forget-me-nots,
you watch my open face in shadowed light,
to candle memory on some lonely night.

After riffs of kisses, strums of love,
in these small things familiarity grows:
your folded coat, red-check shirt on the chair,
discarded nightwear green as shaded grass.

Too many years for me since other loves,
you sing me back inside my flesh, desire.
I reach to hold it closer to my heart
noisy sleep wound round like spider's silk.

It was the *otherworld*, perhaps it was,
and you a *shee* who caught and took me there,
along dim roads beside the scurrying mist
to that wide house beneath sky gorged on stars.

There was a channel white the moon had carved,
into the lake beside your well-locked door,
you wrapped your arms about me from behind
breathed glittering light in sighs from *Bealtaine's* chill.

Your eyes close gentle when you sing old tunes.
I know you see him, Wandering Aengus there.
Fire inside his head burns fierce like mine,
like mine his hands grope blind dark worlds for love.

Now across the world I sleep alone,
restless for your voice at midnight still,
skin-hunger gnawing at me in my dreams,
from which a faery comes to bring your form.

From each untangled tress, drop sun's gold fruit,
in his stretched hand, your face, your smile, your laugh;
his breath, your scent in tendrils round my lips,
his cheek, wrapped curve of you asleep along my back.

Yet is it magic or my own be-twitching need?
Are you forever young on distant shores,
or mortal, have forgotten me so soon,
among pink fallen dust of cherry trees?

– reference to Yeats' poem 'The Song of Wandering Aengus'
 – *shee*: fairy in Irish
 – *Bealtaine:* (pron, *bal*-tin-uh) old Celtic festival on May Day, the coming of
summer and the light, when thoughts turn to love and fertility

Hunger

to my mother

Life for you was a long hunger,
your own *Gorta Mór*,
its litany of regret
a taste-of-ash longing on your tongue.
'Just when I was getting it right,'
you said to me in your dying.
I wonder at the inheritance of yearning,
the small burning gene that carries it pulsing,
sets us adrift on a wave of wandering;
untidal, never beached at shore.

I imagine it began in Ireland:
your grandfather's leaving with
his mother, his two brothers –
five brothers and sisters buried, and a father.
Leaving with the scent of green in his mouth
that drink could never wash away.
They never talked about it, left us no clues.
Every spare detail I have
is dug slowly from rocky corners of strange fields,
tracking a faded footprint for only part of a story.

We were taken off country, though still unborn;
melancholy the replacement for interrupted memory,
connections severed.
Migrants in our own souls, hearts forever refugee,
our bones cry out for the light to go on
in the yellow windows of home.
You went there with me, you knew it rang familiar.
Ever since I knew that place my heart has made this crying sound.
Perhaps it was Ireland and not yourself
as handed me so much loss.

– *An Gorta Mór*: the Great Hunger, the great famine in Ireland 1845-49

Spring in the Blue Mountains

Day here is easing into summer gently;
shirt I wear of fabric so light
as not to be fabric at all,
rather a leftover cloud
caught into its own weave,
cumulus stowaway tardy at leaving from a 'mountain day'
when mists were lolling in streets,
cluttering gutters with straps of white brocade,
rolling into our mouths,
an ingression of sensual organza.

We were eating clouds,
taking them into our lungs,
scooping them out from indented stone,
trying to capture them behind sycamore and oak
in this garden too silent for birds.
Night would bring thunder to pound cliffs,
lightning to seek out ironstone veins
shooting up static of cloud-making,
the secret entrance to the blue;
the too-blue for a word.

Not the blue of forget-me-nots;
not blue of window frames on Samos, or the Aegean sea;
not the blue of sapphires my mother dug out of crumbling earth,
my father cut into starlight;
not the blue of Arctic ice on dusk meeting a smudged line of ocean;
not a searing Australian heaven in summer
steaming out of hot tarmacadum;
not hyacinths;
not Mexican blue for which Frieda Carlo lusted;
not the blue of your eyes deep in hunger.

A word on clouds

i.m. Harry Phillips, photographer, 1873-1942, Katoomba.

I have been walking with shadows again, busy in 'the service of clouds'.
My task is to blend the two, wraith and illusion, and in so doing,
find the cipher to make a language of clouds; notate their mother-tongue,
so passers-by will no longer be lost in their misty ignorance.

Clouds are humble. From that great union of earth and water
they have been set apart as diviners of the future;
prescient, they allow form to reveal our coming frailty,
but being torn and solitary, they lack the community of tongues.

Round and plump, the brilliance of white Cumulus
stuns blue of skies into deepness, watching the sun's yellow warp
filter its way into indigo through gaseous fluid enveloping the earth.
Tentacled Cirrus trails its filamentous limbs across these crags

stroking trees into green, fingering shredded haze into crevices
between the Three Sisters. Their nibs scratch spirit drawings into the sky,
those images caught at the corners of sketches
a painter might have turned toward their blind eye.

More difficult though are Stratus banks that thicken like fog,
phantom Niagaras thundering in billows over Narrow Neck,
sucked from Megalong Valley, bunched thick before
plunging soundless to flood Jamison Valley with ivory spume.

Harry Phillips was good at it: recording the language of clouds.
He sent his photograph *War Clouds* to the King of England in 1911,
foretelling World War One with his interpretation of cloudscapes,
their astute sense of history, their yearning towards peace.

Balancing high on barely-accessible ledges with shouldered tripod,
he would wait, and wait with the patience of clouds, tasting wispy floss.
Love seeping into his plates, he captured the children of clouds
iced in waterfalls, cascades; the Bridal Veil calcified; the snowy flesh of

frozen trees, their dark twigs a converse of x-ray limbs.
Decades he spent in their shadows, places of vapour;
in bright-white night-skies, airy filaments of cloud wrapping moonbeams,
struggling with their silver shatter, to articulate legible signs.

– John Ruskin on landscape painting, used by Delia Falconer in her novel,
The service of clouds.

Shadow dreaming

There is a vernacular of shadows
ciphered from an Auslan of clouds,
sweeping, fingering, gesturing.
They are confused, the tongues of shadow,
broken off when the Tower of Babel fell.
You have to watch closely, listen with eyes,
and not be distracted by the ivory sails
of barques scudding above in the blue.

Seeming insubstantial, these shots of black have burnt holes
into the valleys below, blotching out
their mossy sheen, their cumulus of leafy olive
fallen into the charcoal dark.
These burnings are prescient messages,
signs for tribes that have lived here before
but those stories and the people who read them
were lost in long-ago white storms.

Scarp's orange glow fades under their path.
Disposed into gray, they shrivel into background.
Stone is deaf to the idiom of shadows
even when continents are drifting apart
and foreign predators prowl across the lowlands;
tigers, lions, and those who carry weapons in their hands.
Armies are gathering in large and larger battalions,
phalanx after phalanx darkening the slopes.

When a draught of air rises mercurial from the falls,
a tumult of angels come galloping down
trumpets blazing,
crochet and quavers from their blast racing after
small remnants of patrols seen rushing the ridges.
Down, down the Seraphim fly
and before a moment,
splatches on the face of these boundless hills
fray and disappear in another triumph of wind;
the sky left pure, wide as an innocent eye.

Dangers of light

Salt-cold from the sea
my feet are suddenly small,
recalling childhood nights with
prawning net heaving in my hand,
lake water lapping my chilled thighs,
moon above, an uneven pudding.
I held the lantern high as a child's arms could,
peering into the lake's uncertain depth,
adrenaline hit sucking at my gut, tight with excitement.

They seemed to love the light.

Tonight the squid boats
candesce fluoro-white off Belongil beach,
halogen sharp on a blue-black sea.
At home, they are stationed off Zeally Bay
gathering the horizon in their wake
its dark ermine a thrill along the cape of net.
From a distance the boats seem to hold out long oars,
as if Roman slaves in their bellies
are ready to pull them towards battle.

But things are easier now, mechanical.

Fingers of tide, their nails sunset-pink,
are sliding up this limb of beach.
The creek's lips are shocked cerise.
Flickers of white strobe crackle like static from lighthouse glass
before a sudden boost through its clear pane.
Tower stark-ivory, no-one touches it now in the dark.
It hears no night words,
no rustle of sheets as the keeper settles to bed,
no rough hand slapping the wall on his way upstairs.

Squid come for it too –

light; the lonely, silent, cold light.
They are creatures caught in desire for it, lust for it,
each with their three hearts beating frantic, as
they hurry out of their dim warmth toward it,
toward steel arms and webbed fingers of the fleet
whose net wings are pinioned to the idea of fishing,
casting light before them,
siren promise of redemption,
silver angels of death.

Hibiscus

Against uncertainties of night
that in yesterday evening's dark
struck lightning into the grass before them,
golden hibiscus flowers fold into themselves.

Pink-arteried, their undersides seem vulnerable,
clench round vibrant hearts
to resemble dead blooms,
claret stamens withdrawn for safety in this early dawn.

Through the glass pane I watch its flowers,
flutes of yellow, opening with tenderness
in their sweet offering to the sun
whose own bloom draws them forth.

We live too far apart for daily loving,
for lips murmuring moist on skin.
Circumstance of distance makes our practice
the intimacy, the buoyancy, of voice.

Through wayward trees,
across the border and salty bite of deep water,
in all the shared ways we feel alike
care has found a way to hold us both, together.

So I shiver in this sleepless morning,
that draughty phone call blowing through me still –
unprivate, overheard, your words a whisper, absent of attention
shadow-sounds merely, vacant of you.

I learn the lesson of not doing, of not speaking,
observing my hibiscus, furled in against hurt,
waiting for the warm rays of your voice
to return to me, along coaxial night.

Lost lover of mine

Close on me now, waking I feel your sigh damp along my nape.
Aftershave lingers,
or is it just freesias in the blue vase,
their throats sinning colour,
the dark and light of it – carmine, cerise, bright yellow,
their gladness untarnished at sweet opening day.

Dream so full of you it spills into the fringed light of dawn.
I carry it into the open yard
where rain has spoiled the dew.
Your skin still burns my bare arm.
Inside my wrist your tongue's wet imprint
blurs the boundary of sleep with sunlight.

Now the years number three. I do not keep count.
Sleep is the store place of reckonings.
Yearnings are vast there;
grottoed caverns swim with unspoken longings best forgotten,
trickster unconscious peddling its case
for inching fantasy into the broken light of day.

Sometimes these dreams
in the blackberry-bramble dark
make me believe you think of me still.
Then citrus dawn stings away
shape-shifter night,
blank sky carrying no reflection.

Dark emerald velvet of old drapes,
that field where we lay down.
You gave me your sweater later in the chill.
It had soaked up all that verdant colour
and where it touched my skin, you passed through,
leaving a green whispering in the blood.

Oh lover of mine, oh dark loss,
where can I put you down outside my dreaming?
Among wandering ache of body
or in the mirage of my heart, searching, searching.
I cannot find the well of forgetfulness.
Overgrown, it keeps those waters from me.

If only I had the tongue of Hafiz
to make you my rejoicing god; put *there* my keen desire.
I could give you song without grief and
all my lust would be pure.
Oh lover of mine, lost, take memory away with you;
all it takes is one scarlet slash.

Hafiz: Sufi poet, Iran 1320-1389

This moon

on the Great Ocean Road from Apollo Bay

Day's end lingers faintly in the belly-flat bay.
Leaving, I drive up, into gum forest
pressed hard and tight into the land.
Road winding, traces the huddle of hills
folded along cliffs that dive
crashing ginger red ochre into the waves below.
Beyond – the big, big sea.

Out there, on the horizon, a
tangerine full moon rises from raven-shot clouds
in a sky feathered kingfisher-blue.
Barely there, its sigh of henna haze is a light veil dropped
in the blackening sky, then lost,
to float orangy wet on ripples close to shore.

If I had just woken
I would think it dawn, and
wonder where sunrise had gone.

Another curve in the road, the sky is black, bereft.
Then behind a harem grille of cloud,
the moon, embarrassed to have risen flushed and unclothed,
reassembles her garb,
cloaks herself in silvery sheath over
shadowy nipples, purpled cleft,
to shine singular, a little haughty, above the turrets.
Beneath, only a pool of talc
on the softened skin of sea.

Two bends more, all light is gone.

Moon, moon –
how lonely the dim road is
without you.

David – stone and flesh

I Michelangelo finding David

Florence 1501-1504

How is it that you loved him so swiftly
as he stopped naked to wash dust from his pores
after a day scaffolding?
Leaning towards the water barrel:
the arched bridge of his ribs,
the taut thigh, haunch streaked with sweat,
one smooth buttock bruised purple from a fall of timber.

So clearly his body formed under your hands.
The block of marble, flawed and useless to others,
welcomed your sharp tools in the braille of yearning,
shaking, uncertain, carving your longing into his belly;
his soft groin; those veins threaded wrist to fingers, navel to heart;
hands sluicing water onto his chest
its tawny furze, nipples lip-pink.

Lovelier than the grimy original
who walked senseless, unseeing,
not attending to your hungry shadow halted in the archway,
this image of him is perfected –
at least to hold that in stone – David to your Jonathan,
and all your passing youth, your mirrored pride there,
humbled by his carelessness.

You could drink the stinging salt behind his lids,
finger the tight-packed spring of his curls,
furl and unfurl them around your thumb,
and know everything there is to know
until you die:
remembrance of youth and its loveliness;
all folly, all wisdom; and love, forever passing by.

II David in stone

Galleria dell'Accademia, Florence 2004.

Stumbling through streets, narrow and waist-pinched
in a city of bridges,
dragging two young sons, I am snappy, irritated by searching.

Suddenly, fumbling with space under this high dome,
I am stilled by a smooth perfection in you
towering unclothed above,
your gaze turned from me.
There is no breath, no heart striking time.
Yet sensuality runs tributaries in your veins,
thieved away into stone,
thrilling
through the skin of marble.

An eager mouth could trace your topography:
rising the length of firm calf,
scrotum-teased thigh,
belly curved to receive a cheek,
ribs taut with the lung's cage.
In your groin the crevice of desire
yet to bloom,
in your hand, the sinuous veins of fresh life
caught waiting.

If ever chiselled flesh invites tongue,
if ever youth's flush invites the kiss,
you, stand ready.

Yet this is not a day for thoughts of lovers,
boys nagging at my side.
We walk around you,
calm acceptance in your profile, fleeting,
absent from your direct gaze.
There, full lips, slightly open, begin their understanding
of what is being asked;

of what being anointed now means –
no small matter it is by God.

Foolish you must have seemed
facing Goliath shimmering in bronze mail.
Foolish to stand naked without shame,
only a shepherd's leather sling
swinging loosely from your shoulder –
and five round stones.
Certainty in God is your sheen and girdle;
invisible armour, the skin of faith,
sleek as an eel's.

Your hand
curls around,
the cool, blunt stone of death.

The moment moves in
as it might to all young men
balancing on the ledge of change, life unravelling.
Your frown quivers a furrow of regret
for what is about to come:
death, the scissor sword and heavy head,
sudden burden of your fame,
a kingdom, wars, the wives, the children –
but Jonathan.

And I, who have sons
pull them close suddenly, and shiver
for what made you a man.
Neither spear, nor javelin, nor sword, I hope;
not all the killing.
This instant perhaps: this reflection.
This hesitation of inhaled breath, this concern
before the measured act.
Never the act itself.

Unblemished,
here is the last moment of innocence
captured in cold rock.

The weight of a man

Dragonflies are shimmering,
mating in the green breeze over the ocean.
Their wings levitate delight, hovering – then dart.
Sometimes they fall exhausted into vivid blue,
the wine-stain of rock, dark beneath.
Mostly, they shiver, light as threadbare gauze.

But I want you heavy on me.
Lay yourself warmly here,
cradle these shoulders firm inside your arms,
heart stealing into my globe of ribs;
breath laced into clavicle; sacs between my thighs.
This holding under the press of you loosens longing.
No need even for love –
the weight of your body alone, will comfort.

Dead-end

Honeyed moon golden in the sky
twists away shadows from
maturing in late dusk.

Wrists of the callistemons
are dripping with flowers
that stain the driveway scarlet.

Beside them white lilies stalk
the tangled yellow hope
of prone mimosa.

I am glad I never showed you my scars:
that at least is private under the
blunt ice of your silence.

uncertain life

for Jennifer Harrison
ever after cancer

How can others know about this lightless place,
surviving torment of the trickster flesh,
where dormant chaos hides tomorrow's face,
where courage holds our hearts and fear our guess?

If I could gather plucking one by one,
whole bright stars from heaven's dark-blue snare,
would their white fearsome light freeze out the sun,
or burn away this silver sadness that we share?

The waiting

Sea-rusted sun rising,
night is a castaway in yellow dawn.
Everything depends
on the slant of light on your face this day,
turned towards me
or turned away.

Waiting, choral filaments of breath,
taut and silent,
prepare the hymn my heart will sing:
'amidst encircling gloom', hope's flare dowsed
beyond a glimmer; or, broken open, ablaze and golden,
love's burnished hallelujah.

Blue line

Between these breasts,
in horseshoe arch,
its oxbow raised toward the throat,
one blue vein, delicate but firm,
sinuates
between the soft ripe ache of desire
and rose studs of nipple,
one askew now, forever burnt pale.
This dark thread curls above my heart,
over the first starry compass point
of tattooed blue dots
that mark radiation limits for next time,
should there be one.

One blue vein, curved,
like the beach worms I threaded onto hooks
as a child, an adult,
casting above the weeded waves
to plonk into the channel
on an evening beach needy for the catch.
In the mirror I watch it pulse the heart's song,
carry the breath's freight,
and wait anxious
in this anticipation, this hope for luck,
for allure to work
one last time, before dusk
along the beached blue line.

Almost abundance

Sunset becalmed at Ballyvaughan
overlooking Galway Bay,
two white swans
glide among low-tide stone in the harbour,
green moss silent by brown weed
content to lie webbed.
Unmoving embrace, rock is exposed all round,
mountains of it bald gray
where once massive oak forests were felled for English ships.
A great stillness –
day at anchor –
as night at least is breathed into being,
slow though it is in coming,
without hurry.

Into these hard hills,
tunnels were carved by water in ceaseless motion.
We saw bear bones five thousand years old
that once warmed indented stone there in Aillwee Cave.
We walked those tunnels nearly two kilometres in,
turned off the lights.
Absolute, the pitch blankness,
no upheld hand could scratch its face with light.

Solitude blinks at me now across the waters,
the moment motionless.
Sun's trailed memory hangs cayenne in the clouds,
held breath of a kiss unspent.
Unsubtle it is, this lonely skin aching,
touch suspended, you forever unmoved,
the rock's holding not quite enough.

Remember the Tin Man

Wizard of Oz: 'I think you are wrong to want a heart. It makes most people unhappy. If you only knew it, you are in luck not to have a heart.'
Tin Man: 'That must be a matter of opinion. For my part, I will bear all the unhappiness without murmur, if you will give me the heart.'

You have to know what you're doing
I suppose,
when you lean so far into the curve,
bike tempted to the horizontal,
rider and machine colluding
synchronous in the gamble,
yellow ochre cliffs crushed to rock below
in nature's Colosseum,
ocean bellowing for a bit of colour,
lusting for damage, for broken bones,
for blood's claret across the snowy flesh of foam.
That's courage I guess.

The roadside is junked with wattle.
A blowpipe of sunlight
has shot its cheerful spray of gold haphazard, unpatterned,
among the metal grey trunks and dusty olive leaves,
so that while it shimmers with a thrill of joy,
it has no centre, flowers cast away.

In the distant hills,
heads of eucalypts tightly packed
clump like brain coral or rocks gloved in cunjevoi,
that if pressed under childhood's feet, might
squirt a miasmic iron stain of Australian green.

The uncracked sky floats,
slick of blue ice across a water-barrel in winter.
Beneath it, frozen, I hold my breath
searching for a break through which to gasp.
Clouds huge and black are pumped in,
arriving from the red heart, dry and alien.
I'm settling for the edges of country
clinging to this serpent road, vacant beaches.
I've done this trip once before, babies asleep in the back,
fondling cancer in my chaotic breast.
Is that the map memory now under the wheel
drawn with the squid-ink of depression,
rising from the seabed of the soul,
Atlantis of the lost?

Each morning I swallow little pink happiness pills,
only strong herbs
to film over the ache with a cling-wrap of amnesia.
But now instead of the sad heart, everything is scattered.
On the way out,
my soul forgot to leave behind its thread of words –
its lovely gift, its lovely curse.
The trail is cold and dead inside this labyrinth.
Just the bike riders to follow,
their broad backs, strong thighs;
and the fool's gold bolled-bright among the leaves.

Remember the Tin Man.
I must go back   and find my heart.

Twisted

Up close, at eye level, it's ink black,
no – beyond black, terminal black.
Around the muscle of its own clumped hemp
a cord of rope twists sinewy, worm-veined.
Encircling, it spirals
round the twist,
with its charmed snake-body,
my eye fixed on it, fascinated.

Lovely rope. Lovely.
My soft fingers caress
its tough fibre,
grip its knotted ends hard
in an exercise to ropen biceps.
You could link that rope together,
you could noose it.
It wouldn't snap.

Its corded belt coils
down into my hands,
an acrobat descending, twirling
in a writhe of suppleness and strength.
These are hard days,
pitchy, blurred.
Outside the gym window,
there's only shadow on the wind.

Inside black: therapy

for Wendy, with thanks

March 2003.

Anxiety burrows constantly.
It seems impossible to continue, and to end.

There is someone in my therapist's waiting room today.
That's never happened in six months.

I don't speak to visitors
in the house on Princess Street.

I might get
answers I can't understand.

I might get
assumptions of familiarity.

They might be taking my place.
I might have been forgotten.

March 2005

But you don't forget us, my Dead Mother and I,
balancing your golden crown above the familiar face of a stranger;
you, to whom I owe everything and leave nothing.
You'll walk soon, down the ash-carpet corridor of my past
leaving footprints I might need again.
I'm slicing my heart apart from the dead weight of her cargo;
but you too, you'll have to be left behind.

It's time to leave home.

I feared sometimes you had become my fixer, my dealer.
Or worse: you stood in my way;
you were her pimp, and I would be sold out;
or worse,

that I'd lost her to you, in you,
that her voice was yours, and
I couldn't trust you to take my part, hear me.

Maybe, I thought, I can't leave you – you, who are always here with her?

At first, I mistook the ocean's surface for depth
before a wrenching storm tore it open.
Far, far beneath, through the blur of fish
there seemed what might be sunken treasure.
I had to plunge deep, scratch and dig into the gloomy floor to discover
first, the jammed lock, then, the rusted key,
while you held a lantern high above juggling waves,
clamouring white palms slapping water against rocks, and
her voice above the sirens telling me:

'The search will take you away, not set you free.'

In the very dark, down where giant squid squirt fluoro,
antithesis to everything above,
murkish visions draw themselves out from the too-fluid past.
There are fish there, you know, with barely a head,
white, thin and grotesque –
species created that way merely by the absence of light.
Some seemed to wear my smile, my face.
I had to find a new way of breathing there.

I had to snatch at bubbles, sieve saline crystals, listen.

Underwater, sounds can be distorted,
but I loved the crinkle-static of fish crunching on coral,
small teeth grinding, nipping my feet as if I were weed.
And when I kicked out, dove up against the weight of water –
meniscus above a bulging eye-lens –
this new voice struggled out of a thinning depth
gurgling, full of salt; single words, unjoined, unbound with sense,
no necklace yet of knotted pearls.

But that will come in the end – out of these stinging lips.

You met her first in her red shroud.
She didn't like you very much, remember?
She sat with her hands in my lap, her rings on my fingers;
spoke with my voice, laughed at her own cleverness.
You waited many months; you never hinted you might know
where we were going, what it might mean.
You listened; you heard me say it.
You did it so well, I heard it myself: wrong was done against me.
Hurt, invaded, betrayed; I was abandoned to the Dark.

It was a long time. It was a long time ago.

It might have been too late.
Gills were forming; there wasn't much time.
Breath was water or air?
Without malevolence, she had taught me the song by rote:
one flesh, one mind, one heart, one life; and no-one to love us at all.
But you waited, you always had faith.
You must have hoped – if you didn't know – that in here
there was the core of someone who might be myself.
If I could just swim up. Or down? I had to get clear.

I don't like confusion – that's what is saving me.

Just the laying of it down for her now – life's prismatic ambivalence:
hard dark stories; ones with smiling and light;
a set of scarred veins in memory's heart, and above,
the peach-smooth other cheek.
Loving her the way I did, the way I do,
the worst has to be caught safe in the unbreathed silence, for now.
My father says, 'Some things are best left unsaid.'

The work feels almost done.

II

Dead Mother Poems

a selection

Adhesion

2005

I had to do this, mother.
It got too dark and lonely here with you, living underground,
only the sound of the earth
as it rubs against the walls turning in its sleep.
I had to do it; the rush is on me.
One red angel stands brushing light from the door,
her hollow wings whirring like flight.
I have to fix it now, or stay lost.

I'm so tired. I can't carry you any further,
my body frenzied, it fizzes like gunpowder in a catherine wheel.
This weight.
This weight makes me weary;
and the Dark so heavy.
They don't get that do they,
how exhausted it makes us in this lightlost maze?
Is that you or me?

If I can just slip this skin,
rise out of this flesh,
the load will be left behind, won't it; fall into ashes, feather-light
crushed with the bone, and the sad, sad heart?
There's a stain here. Can you see that; can you?
Can you hear me calling you?
Look at this stain.
You tell me where it came from.

You or I? How can I tell?
Who owns this voice? Who speaks?
What did you do here to make one mind out of two
then leave me alone?
I know how you feel.
I am how you feel. You grew into me.
I am the Mandrake plant;
this unearthing, my long screaming.

Original tar baby
I am stuck to you without feathers to fly
coming cauled with your own childhood night.
What happened to my skin?
You adhered to it; no borders.
Nothing contained me, nothing held.
Everything flowed away into you
and your tide rushed back in me.

I was born old.
I was born responsible
mother forever young.
Never grown, how you clung.
It must have frightened me.
I was a child, my shoulders never strong enough,
pallbearer for your dead life.
You were my burden, my debtor's note.

I've come for the cure.
Soon, I'll see boundaries,
tall gates; an arranged toll.
Once words are down here, you'll be on the outside.
They do it to conjoined twins.
It's bound to hurt.
It's sliding along my spine now –
the filleting knife.

Part One

Dying notes

August 1989 – January 1990

I am, I am

First time surgery, 1989

You're in surgery, and I'm fearful for you.
Life is about to change, and us with it.
I'm about to see myself in your mirror.
I'm the one who is about to understand
how deep my love can go for you.
You're the one who is going to let me love you,
the one whose body will be sliced,
a bag to replace your bowel.
I'm the one who will help to get that right for you.
I'm the one who will have to tell you.

After all the years of our torture,
cutting each other, careless,
as if it goes on forever and will somehow cleanly end,
a step off the kerb could have done it,
leaving me the hole that nothing fills
the need to say again and again.
'I am, I am.
I am not you.'

Your part in the digging,
your part in the carving, was long ago.
Someone should have told you then:
'Be a grown up – nothing terrible happens.'
But that won't change; won't ever be untrue, undone.
I wanted you to say: 'Yes, I did it, I'm sorry.'
But, I'm about to be the one who will never hear it,
who will have to forgive.
You're about to find out
how deep my love can go.

Tightrope walking
12 January 1990

You were big with undelivered dreams
when I was born thirty-eight years from this day.
They cheated you with their promise of happiness
if you would be a good girl inside four walls.
Friends write now of kindness.
The fruit on your trees are many,
buds loading branches
heavy, with unfinished growth.

Luminous, your eyes unshade a child's innocence.
Joy opens into you with the scent of rosebuds.
All your life you railed: against him, against me,
against chopped up moments of chance.
Steady and fearless now,
you burn that parched scroll with its litany of hurts,
forget the patois of regret,
dumb with delight in simple things.

I give you a cloth marigold on a long-necked stem,
that by some clever mechanical twist dances to music,
moves its face towards sound.
Petunia, you call her,
red and yellow heart-shaped sunglasses, intimate smile.
She leans toward you to kiss your cheek as you speak to her,
set her dancing to *Aida*'s Triumphal March.

You grow heavier, liver ballooning as if to float you up.
Exhaustion grinds my bones,
balancing doctors' opinions on my head,
a basket of stones you are learning to notice.
We go to Circus Oz. You resent the hired wheelchair.
Naked young bodies flaunt their skill with trumpets,
airborne, rainbow-bright.
'I wouldn't have missed this for the world,' you whisper, worn.
I will keep you alive by distractions. 'Not long now,' they say.

Dying notes I

12-14 January 1990

This dying business is such hard work.
I ask doctors to burden me with truth.
They do: 'It could be any moment.'
We've stopped them.
Dad stands in the kitchen, still husband
three years after schism, making tea.

Friends visit. It's one big party here: the laughter,
rooms overflowing with blooms that rival an Amsterdam flower barge.
I take you to have your hair done. It costs.
Mirror confused, daily you recede into your mother, and
I into you, going grey, as you did when she died.

I cut your fingernails, hand resting dust-light in my palm.
Even in death the body grows, unaware
inside there are forces at work that oppose its purpose.
I wipe you fresh; wash soiled clothes and sheets.
He cleans the carpet you stain, our anchor man.
You lean on me, hug me tight, smile childlike:
'You're a good daughter.' Stunned, I trip.

At night I sleep on your floor
waking each time you struggle for the bathroom.
'Amazing,' you say, 'like living with a baby,
you seem to know the moment I'll wake before I do.'
Doctors say something else is keeping you alive.

I know it's the attention, just you at the centre.
You want more of that before you die.
Generous in your dying, you share it with me
allow all ministrations, opening to my comfort,
listening finally
to this last love serenade.

Contradictions

He made grandfather clocks out of red cedar,
after you left him, and he stood quietly
in the long years of rearranging rooms, cleaning cupboards,
replacing worn carpets you'd hated,
taking out walls
like he was reshaping the home he'd built
for a better fit now; until,
in my father's house,
there are many empty drawers.

You were always wanting one, but your house echoed silence.
One stood in my brother's hallway, and in mine;
made with his dusted hands that cut the wood,
borer-proofed the frame,
set the mechanism that needs winding each week, reliably.
You have to attend to a clock with pendulum,
weights in balance with time.

Now you are dying three years after you left him.
I'm here with you making carrot juice, and
he's moved in with us,
his kindness the balm we both need
binding the three of us,
tending wounds with his humour that once landed a sting
but you both suddenly remember you share.

He doesn't say much: never one for words.
He brought the clock,
set it up outside your bedroom door.
Four times a night you wake, cancer alive in your liver,
a nocturnal creature.
You lie waiting 'til the hour comes round,
to know the time by counting chimes.
It drives you mad on the indefinite quarter and half-hour.
'I love that clock,' you say, eyes wet, 'even though it drives me crazy.'

Shutter open

Some moments don't need a frame.
Your hand unsteady
drops the one glass of French champagne
you worry might harm your liver.
I help you change and start again.
But that's not the picture.
When I tell you then, four days before you die, 'I'm pregnant',
your hand is surprised by strength clasping mine,
fingers berthed between them in safe harbour.
'Now you'll have someone to look after you,
the way you've looked after me.'
Bright rafter of sunlight.
I am captured by its sweep.

Your face is gathering itself in.
Jaw and cheekbone pronounced, your profile thinly fine
sheened-sallow; still not yielding its lovely so-smooth skin.
'A little of you will stay with us now,' I offer,
fearful my sadness will spike loss into it.
Blue flame of your eyes, fading and low,
suddenly fires into radiance,
Big London flicking on the Christmas lights – and it's this:
you turn towards my father,
raising those eyes spilling blue joy, say to him clear as a teardrop,
'and a part of you too, my one true love.'

Dying notes II

18–25 January 1990

'Pre-comatose,' they say. So many intricacies in dying:
your rosebud embroidery on our dressing-table doilies, lace tea-cloths;
learning to peg out washing in categories, neat colour groups;
jaundice, liver failure, making an abacus of your sleeping breath.
Surprising me then, you wake refreshed before the next slump.
As I leave the room – 'straighten your shoulders!'– sharp as ice.

My brother comes finally, helpless with his set jaw.
You have been waiting, you have been angry.
Now everything is forgiven, set to rights.
His blond hair is shining in your bedroom light.

You are big; sphere of your belly heavy with fluid.
What do you think of in the night? I know your spirit seeks God.
Is that what brings out this grace, this consenting peace?
'I'm not afraid to die,' you say, 'I'm ready,
they are waiting for me, but I'm sorry to leave you.
I never loved anyone the way I've loved you.'

I suck on sleep like a hungry child but the milk is dry.
My eyes seem always open, gaps in the face.
We shower together so I can hold you up,
yellow all over, your mound collapsed.
You fade away from me, voiceless;
only the slow fall of your eye, slackening smile.
Suddenly you're back! Death is a see-saw.

I walk the beach for strength, a strawberry half-moon after dawn:
the cruelty of sun, gold on a blue sea,
the cruelty of people leaping between waves,
the cruelty of old women salt-white, boisterous in the spume.

all through the night

all night the sea has lain with the moon
generous,
spread her favours to your soft bed
sleepless,
you are counting stars and waiting
oblivious;
you think, I know, there might yet be some time.

all night beside I have lain with the moon
hopeful,
now I stand in dawn's salt ripples
watching,
all her white light from plenteous waters
draining,
her waves loose-girdled with her silver sigh.

into me slow I draw it from the deep
shimmering,
send it by sheer will upstairs to you
channelling,
demeter, persephone confused here
clinging,
dark sail at dawn I see it – pass on by.

let us talk of bodies similar
changing,
your hands, your hips are mine and now a death
arriving,
flesh is leaving you; muscle, wrinkles
departing,
leaving here, the child that you once were.

all night the moon has lain inside the sea
embracing,
spread her fingers to your soft bed
caressing,
you are counting stars in grace and courage
knowing;
you think now we might almost be on time.

The moment open

26 January 1990

You sleep the coma slumber of one leaving;
blood trickles gently from the corner of your mouth;
body closing down. Simply that.
Daylight comes while I hold you, kiss you; sails are full.

Your grandfather clock chimes six. I know you hear it.
Your hand inside mine is warm,
a pulse so quiet it seems to deny breath,
yet the chest remains on subtle duty.

Tear-drenched, my body is fluid, borderless.
I read aloud your favourite passage in Corinthians:
'Love is patient, love is kind ... love never fails ...'
Over and over this mantra,

until, in the space before silence, suspended words
evolve into flickering motes, drifting swiftly away.
All sound absent,
death holds the air becalmed.

I see it happen then, as surely as light changes
when cloud dissipates, moving to release the sun.
Pink sea-mist rises in a sigh
as day opens to the unblinking blaze.

Mourning
March 1990

We have become an Estate.
Bills come addressed to it.
I swell in the middle,
think of your body, balloon-tight with fluid.
Fear grips me – this *is* to be birth?

Holding my belly close I croon to the child to come,
remembering how much you know:
how earth was formed; names of rocks, minerals;
how a diamond is made; to test pearls on your teeth;
why tides love the moon so faithfully, they follow her.

You know about continents moving;
Gondwana; majesty and terror in dinosaurs.
You can ride the Niles of history,
transport us to Tutankhamun's tomb.
You know about being pregnant.
Do you know how I can do this without you;
how a daughter can step into the space
her mother leaves behind her?

May

People expect recovery.
They think it should finish. It might never.
I call your number, though I disconnected it myself.

Everything breaks me open:
scent on your clothes, Essence of Absence;
black onyx compact with diamanté bow,
its face powder ready to pat onto your cheeks,
not quite you, but familiar, the dust of it.

Ash, ash: just a smudge on the sky's blank cheek,
nothing to compare with memory.
Nothing that can snuff out your voice; and in my veins, you still singing.

8 July

Today is your birthday.
What celebration does this allow?
I wear your pearls
I dial your number.
The baby squirms, kicks at me from the deep.

Where are the Screaming Places,
Palaces of Grief

high on cliffs; higher than the world

from which I can shout out hungry loss,
rain down bitter curse,
call up Furies, Harridans, Banshees,
Roar,   Screech,   Wail,
Shred clothes,
Rip hair,

smother myself in ashes, and

Howl
the great Howl:
bellowing echoless across a wasteland
barren of your touch,
all things diminished under
this umbra in the heart –

this rasping desolation of the motherless?

Part Two

The filleting

2003 – 2005

Path out of the labyrinth

Don't think I'm alone with you, mother.
Don't think I haven't prepared.

I have my therapist from Princess Street.
She sits in a chair that's grown roots into the earth.

She doesn't acknowledge you, red angel in your searing fury
She doesn't know you, fear you, or need you.

She is my medium, my bridge, my protector.
I'll have you out there now, where we both can see you.

I started this. I wanted to clean out my gallery of wounds.
But beyond that twisting corridor's end, the star chamber – and you.

You taught me lessons, I see that now: I separate, and the Dark is unending.
Punishment follows: you will be hurt.

I have that power. It rages beyond a hurricane's spiral.
It binds strong as spider's silk.

I am so powerful I bring death to those I let go of.
Everything falls apart if I don't hold on.

You weep. But I know what happened in the kitchen: a broken glass;
who dropped it. I was turning away. You brought your foot down.

Blood was your scarlet smile; guilt my rough crown.
But I saw it – deliberate – naked arch stepping onto it, the slit grin.

Don't think you can get me that way now.
This bond of mutual clinging has frayed itself to freedom.

Whose is this voice? Mine or yours?

Inside myself, that's where I always have company.
When you are gone how lonely it will be in here.

Conversations, dialogue, are endless here;
sad, critical, endless here.

But I can't give you up yet, you know that;
you told me that a long time ago.

Whose voice will I speak, how will I know it is mine?
You burrowed so deep. See these hands: they are yours; these eyes, this smile.

Without you, I fall away; the Dark has no boundary –
it travels round the earth like an ocean.

As I come near the horizon, I find it only delusion,
imagined in the mirage of dawn I'm chasing.

I climbed the Tour de Belém near Lisbon; up top watched
Vasco da Gama sailing off the edge of the world.

What courage. What surprise when they discover,
it just keeps going round and round, like the Dark.

Cloned from your depression, even my pen is carved from it.
Without it, what would there be to feel?

Chronos swallowed his children at birth until one rose up against him.
I hunt down my emetic potion. Leave me so I won't have to use it!

But I miss you still. I long for you.
There is not enough salt for you; my tear-bottles overflow.

Fifteen years dead. Yield me up!
If you could not before, help me now, mother.

This maze has me buried deep. I've been lost in here with you.
But my golden-haired witness is holding a thread.

I've come right in – but I'm getting out.

Journey in

I

Branded into me,
there isn't a road I can follow
that doesn't return to you.
Here is the back country we travelled as kids.
Smothered in Paterson's curse,
fleshy hills along Olympic Highway
crush its purple velvet into their cleavage,
powder their shoulders,
sherbet their lips and grow wanton with it.
Even the air tastes purple-sweet and musky.

In full view, stringybarks are stripping their trunks.
Bees watch from the flowers and suck hungrily,
legs dusted from the blue-bells' electric stripes
that set fields shimmering into violet
beside patches of lime-yellow canola.
Black cattle, cream sheep, stud a dyed land stretched to breaking
until only unscarred pink sky draws a line.
You'd love it – the excess.
Phoenicians would gaze with envy here, you'd say,
Roman Emperors demand the dye.

This here Wiradjuri country – old place.
But I play Irish tunes anyway
trying to find a word for that citrine-green of the wheat
near Houlaghans Creek,
in a country I find hard to call home.
But you loved it.
You drove us across this vast island year after year,
always on the lookout for adventure, for oddities,
for a real land and a way into it,
for finding what it was you were looking for.

At Cowra, escapee willows press themselves into
the Lachlan's wet meander, its banks crowded with trees

allowed to drink still at the edge,
not cleared away or untangled.
Near Junee, the railway track is my stake
against wandering too far from intention,
from the purpose of the journey.
This is for freedom, isn't it? Not getting lost.

These are towns where the past still lightens the present
even though 'they grow wheat short now.'
Towns where bakeries still make butterfly cakes
that taste of fresh cream; have clock towers that tell time.
Towns with wide streets and reverse parallel parking,
railway stations laced with charm,
huge metal windmills, working.
Towns where old houses are repaired, not pulled down.

Can you hear me yet? Are you listening?
These are places like those in my childhood.
I'm trying to figure how to get from there to here.
I want to say this at the beginning, uncluttered by image,
in case it seems untrue in the end.
I loved you.
It wasn't enough, I know.
But you were my first impossible friend;
my first unrequited love.

II

Embedded in me,
there isn't a road I can follow
that doesn't come back to you.
Tonight the movie *Million Dollar Baby*:
a young woman boxer, dying;
syringe of adrenaline zapping up memories of morphine,
of you at home in the hospital bed I hired.

Hard it was for you to swallow the poppy's draught,
flowering white then crimson on your tongue.
It burned bitter and choking,

until they inserted the slip of butterfly under your skin
flitting its short life away.
I had to spill it in, measuring drops carefully.
I was terrified later that I'd killed you dulling the pain,
but I managed that long before.
I did it from the moment my wheel spokes
sliced the mandala of my life out of your clay.

III

You had a great job in a leather company,
private secretary to the boss, good with the books,
after aeroplane construction in the war,
after your parents' refusal of an education you wanted:
chemical engineer on the railways like your uncle.
With your brilliant maths, your quick mind,
you were sent at fifteen to secretarial college;
safer for a girl, proper. They kept chance from you.

But you made it anyway, climbing, soaring to the top.
Then the fates of the body you resisted for six married years
drew the line, and pregnant, by word of law,
you were forced to leave
disappearing down a funnel of domestic seclusion,
its repetitive post-war drudgery,
its walls, its dim hollow halls.

I've been looking at old photos, scanning your young face
for moments of happiness, for a smile that seemed to say
yes – and, yes, sometimes it shone a flickering lighthouse beam,
or maybe a star's twinkle, core burned out long ago,
its sparkle an after-light, a trickery of distance.

IV

You lost the first one playing hockey.
Lying drugged in hospital,
hearing instruments clinking into a dish,
you thought they were taking him from you 'bone by bone.'

Swamped in guilt you clung to me like a raft
caught on the current of your confusion, chin barely above,
pulling me close, desperate,
all else slipping away.

Tight. Infused with you, I couldn't breathe alone.
But this wasn't what you wanted; or maybe it was;
though not scrabbling hands, the mewling, skirt-clinging child.
Thrusting me off in irritation,
you wandered inland basins dry with despair.
Abandoned in your silence, in the long quiet afternoons,
no friends after school, I knew you needed me in there.
In that loneliness
we threaded together a wet leather harness, drying, shrinking.

In photos grained-grey, you yearn toward an imagined gaze,
face averted from me as you turn me to the lens.
It left the light vulnerable in the face of a child.
Learned by osmosis, sadness seeped through.
It gives me the shine inside my eyes.
I'm sorry I failed to make you happy. I paid for it.
Tenderness breaks me. Lovers leave me alone.

You didn't want me. I got in the way of life.
With Mary Shelley I made my own monster.
No Frankenstein, mine was Home Brand,
stalking inside me, rearing its glandular breath
each time a lover trudges away
his back another tombstone there.

I just haven't tried hard enough, I learned that from you.
But I choose them that way:
their backs already turned, packing when I arrive.
I can hear them now from behind my shut door
out in the sunlight playing,
holding others close, growing love like lotus.
Where was your lesson to me? How to be loved?
Many bequests in this inheritance: diamonds and dust.

Wishes in the night

Today a blue and white perfume spray the size of a large lipstick
fell from your night-velvet evening bag.
It looks like you brought it home from Amsterdam in the seventies
on that long trip with Dad through Europe, before you left him.
Exquisite in its delicate design, its perfect lapis-blaze is the
blue flame of your eyes. Its husk of breath whispers rouge-red and sexy.

I pull off the lid. *Vol de Nuit* by Guerlain is a memory freeze-dried,
scent still intimate as I spray temple, wrist, *décolletage.*
You were so close I could have touched your cheek.
I could hear the swish and rustle
of stiffened long petticoats covered in taffeta organza
as you leaned over my bed to say goodnight before a ball.

You shimmered more lovely than spun ice or
night's beaming smile on a tinselled sea in front of our deck,
Dad so young and handsome in his dinner suit, black bow-tie.
I knew that when I woke in the dawn, our front hall would tumble over itself
with balloons you brought home, squeaking against each other in the crush,
pieces of iced fruitcake wrapped in scalloped paper doilies beside our pillows.

Those were perfect times.

I found a photo of you dancing together in the late fifties,
your face held towards him, smiling over his shoulder,
hand gesturing a joke to the camera for a measure of drink.
Pearls he brought back for you from San Francisco docks
glorify your long neck: a ring of precious moons to light your way,
that no dark thing could trip a stumble.

You two seemed to me more perfect then
than the paper nautilus untouched by ragged storm and grating reef,
beached this New Year's Eve on an apricot haunch of our bay.
Opalescent, unmarked, it felt in my hand as if constructed of air,
its ricepaper skin empty of the life that cast it off along the way.
I was moved by its fragile lightness; its long journey; its flawless intact shell.

The charge

'Greatest show on earth!'
dragging us from our beds in the dark, stars themselves barely blinking.
'Sit here and watch this!'
drawing curtains back from wide lounge windows.
Electrical storm breaking sky's bowl over the sea,
over night's uncracked full moon,
spill of sound tumbling along spindles of light.
'Just giants playing bowls upstairs,' you said sagely.
I believed you. I always did.
Sometimes I thought you made it happen.
You told me I could do anything; I supposed *you* could.
'I couldn't lift a car,' I scorned. *'If you really wanted to, you could!'*

On my tenth birthday we went to Luna Park.
You insisted we ride the Big Dipper,
you in the lead with my small brother.
Everything was falling away; I was shot zooming sideways, and tipping,
tipping: screaming I clung to Dad.
'Don't hold onto me,' he yelled, *'I'm falling out!'*
But you looked back from the front car,
eyes gleaming out of the dusk, grin like the Harbour Bridge:
'Look at those lights will you, just look at that view!'
I was sick all over my birthday dress; we had to go home.

You dragged us over more than half this continent:
country swimming championships, or
collecting sapphires, emerald, topaz, carnelian.
Dad took to faceting them, making jewellery for fun.
We'd find ourselves in dusty inland Murgon
towing camping gear in *Silver Spray*, the boat Dad built out of timber.
People called out to him in desert streets:
'When's the flood coming, mate!'

I remember that dank underground smell of earth-water
while we floated on our backs in a hot bore-pool
one night near Lightning Ridge,
watching, among crowded stars, the first sputnik
steadily cross a bulge of sparkle in an everlasting sky.
'Look at that! Imagine the view from there; imagine that!'
You won a thousand pounds and we went to Norfolk Island,
then Heron and Lord Howe, where you tried to ride a bike.
We have it on silent film – hopeless – always running into a fence or tree,
still grinning at the camera – look at me, look at me.
'See, you can do anything if you want to.'

You wanted to know this country, rubbed it like Aladdin's lamp;
like you were wearing your way in through mere pressure.
Weekends you dragged us around Aboriginal middens,
along the shoreline for shell hunts, through forest walks:
courses you took to feed a mind robbed of schooling.
Then at sixty, you went to university to learn
geography, geology, metallurgy ... and women's studies.
You stayed long enough to prove to yourself you weren't stupid.

You were curious and restless and hungry.
Feet always measuring time before the next adventure,
dragging my boys along beside, I know that in myself now.
With the flooding Dark of you, that came into me too.
That's our Salvation Jane.
I want to ring you now and tell you this bright truth.
I phoned for six months after you died:
dialled your number still hoping for the next surprise;
longing for your voice.

I'm after it now

A child of five outside the tall door at Lane Cove
holding my brother's hand,
with you locked inside.
The door stretched up to heaven,
burnished bronze wood, Goliath's shining shield
blocking out bottle-blue sky.
I knew something was wrong:
you had given us soft drinks.
We never had soft drink.

You called out it would be all right,
the nurse inside with you.
But I knew; I was nearly five.
I knew about doors already.
I knew about the door to your silence.
There was a dark country behind there.
That was your country then,
but I know it better now it's mine.
It goes deep underground through a maze of catacombs.

Voice doesn't follow through soil there.
Nothing that flies lightly, permeates,
and the call of a child is high, a tremulous song,
still free of the future, without the weights of knowledge.
'What are you doing to my mummy!' I screamed.
You needed me.
I knew who had to be in charge; had to protect.
My hands held five small stones.
I never left your door.

Now the old wound gapes:
broken mouth of a giant clam,
deep-slashed well in the berry-dark tangle
beneath feathers, thorns, briars.

I am clearing, scratched and torn, pricked to bleeding.
But deep, this cockeyed pit, with dank viscous waters:
what to do is difficult.
Too late now to lay back the overgrowth,
to walk away.

There is something in there that I need.
I can barely touch it
so crimson,
so large and undone,
ridges of its border difficult to finger –
oozing perimeters layered with sediment,
year on year of grief for your black despair,
your spent life
knotted into mine.

No space for my life,
small girl pressed into an oleander-pink dress
fresh from your crooked needle.
No ear for my voice,
trained to disappear down that funnel.
Ah, maybe that's what I'm searching for.
It looks a long way in,
down. But
I'm after it now.

Red breath: therapy

'It doesn't sound as if she was kind to you?
It sounds hurtful.
Do you still feel her around?'

It's sudden, an explosion's after-haze.
Red at first, a big mist – *Big.*
Inside it, mother, your fire-red angel,
hair vaporous scarlet,
spreads the brume wider,
wider between the therapist and me.

She keeps speaking.
She hasn't seen it.
My hand shoots up, palm pushed out towards her,
a burning shield to ward off speech.
Words, thoughts – you know them, mother –
you don't want them repelling, ejecting you.

Fear rises in a tidal rush, blowhole force;
elevator rockets up out of control;
water is sucked swirling down the drain.
I'm gagging; can't speak properly,
breath enigma,
a language indecipherable.

'Don't do that!' – quick, my voice is rough,
scratched; 'She doesn't like it – my mother –
being talked about like that –
she's really, *really* angry
you have to stop,
you really have to stop!'

Breath an escapee, blast-propelled;
heat sears my inflamed face.
I watch it shimmer between us,
your crimson anger,
your vengeful claim.
My hand keeps its shield up to her words.

I know you're afraid of disappearing;
that wasteland of the invisible.
I won't let her harm you, mother.
I won't let her block you out.
My body is your armour, hold onto me.
I'll hold onto you.   I'll fix it.

In the washroom

I

I wait: feel the moment drag its clubfoot terror:
small – girl – cornered in the dimness of the washroom
walled in by damp cement
and the boy.
A tap drips, staining rust into the concrete basin.
He lunges.
Three fingernails down each cheek
gouge tracks from eye to chin,
bold as finger paintings on white sheets
hanging on the classroom pinboard.

Stumbling home the road is dust.
Westerlies bite my legs.
Skin flaps from its new hinges,
ruts stinging with blood-pink tears.

Next day, the headmaster's shrug:
'Boys will be boys.'

II

My new overcoat was the colour of pressed bluebells:
double-breasted, with a little fur collar
like Princess Elizabeth had as a girl,
the only store-bought beauty
in a childhood of handmade clothes.

I was walking home. She stopped on her bike.
I remember her name.
'What a lovely coat. Can I try it on?'
and so delighted to have something worth sharing,

I held it out in spite of the sniggering breeze, and
knew too late, only by the flick of her sneer.

'Such a lovely coat,' hanging from her hooked finger
above the sludged and muddy drain;
then dragged unprotesting along the gutter,
a rag now with its dirt-brown strobes,
and the sea whispering behind its white hand
on the salt walk home.

III

Every day after school, the tortured gauntlet –
battering, pulling hair, taunting:
girls exclusive in their 'Bluebird Club'.
I had a brooch with two enamel bluebirds
joined by a silver chain, so I never forgot the name.
I tried to take a different road home.
I tried to make a different time,
but they always seemed to know.

'It's because your father has an important job,' you said.
But I knew it wasn't that.
I think they knew something had gone, deep in me,
disappeared, leaving open ground for ravaging.
Something in me was meek, was confused.
They smelt it – and I glowed,
infrared target trapped in the murk of childhood.

IV

You went so often to my primary school
they must have thought you irksome:
arguing, threatening, begging.
Nothing you said made any difference.
Nothing you did made any difference.

You must have felt that cold raging impotence
I saw in you later, when I held you off
flailing, trying to swipe me,
your fists, lost hammers spinning.
At twenty, I was only leaving home.

But in earlier times when I came in from the dusty road,
bullied, astonished, incapable of speech,
bound deeper in our mutual helplessness,
you must have taken me in your arms
to unbruise me, as
I remember them, soothing – the pearl-white wings of angels.

Threads

A scrap gave you away,
wedged beside the garage door where it must have torn
as you pushed leftovers into the bin.
You liked a secret, but were not really good at it.
Cotton with tiny pink and mauve flowers,
it was the same fabric that Santa had used making
Rosebud dolly's sun frock
and I knew Santa didn't live here with us
in all the glorious sunshine of the south coast.

I hid it for three more years and each Christmas Eve
at your parents' house in Concord
battling disappointment, disillusion,
I went to the toilet late at night, just to check,
stumbling through the sunroom,
out along the uneven concrete path under
a thread of moon in the cloud-quilted sky.
With your hand guiding, you'd try to shield my eyes
from the tree and its load of Santa presents,
Rosebud in her dolly splendour beneath.

That doll was decked out all right, every year.
She had ballroom dresses for the foxtrot
shimmering with small pink crystals sewn by hand
over layers of shiny rose petticoats, a stole for cooler nights.
There were day dresses for town, hats, underwear, playsuits,
shorts and suntops with matching skirts for exotic holidays:
all the gorgeous fifties kitout for a princess, a movie star.
You loved glamour, you and Rosebud.
Ava Gardner died the day you did. I thought you'd like that.

You hated sewing; felt you should do it to save money –
we really could not afford store-bought clothes –
and maybe you were right, maybe not.
I remember wrestling those brown-paper patterns,
cutting out shirts on the lounge-room floor,
dog running across it, leaving you furious.
You tried to teach me but I disliked it as much as you did.
You just kept at it, tenacious, with a hint of self-immolation.
I hated wearing them, those flags of old-fashioned style.
With no school uniforms then, they just yelled: 'Hit me.'

Cleaning out your cupboards thirty years on
I found all those doll patterns stacked neatly away.
I thought then about what Christmas had cost you,
what you gave to it; what must have been acts of love.
I saw you then, stooping late at night, secretive,
hands full of stars to sprinkle for a child's delight,
bending over the Singer sewing machine, foot-pedalled,
folding and pinching together those smallest of seams,
stitching hems by hand; sewing on seed pearls, teardrop crystals,
creating this glorious wardrobe; all for a daughter's doll.

still small voice

When the Dark inside me came on and I was eleven
I would walk along the beach alone
thinking the sea looked so big
I could stroke right in,
but would it be cold in there
trying to suffocate by immersion?
Could I hold myself under;
I, who swam so well?
Close, the briny swallow of it. I didn't try though,
then, or since.

No-one was listening.
Your ear was a shell,
its conch boom drowning me out.
My voice was so small to you.
Maybe it seemed to come from a long distance,
and no-one had ever heard yours.
You were still struggling with expectation,
you weren't ready to grow up.
Someone had forgotten your childhood
and now you were stuck.

They said you were a serious child.
You went to see a pantomime,
shocked them when you said: 'The three little bears were lovely,'
the only time anyone recalled you enjoying yourself.
They must have been impressed
because my grandmother told my father after you married,
and my father told me
and I'm telling you
because it must be important if so many people repeat it.

They said your childhood was lonely,
no brothers or sisters;
no friends either, you could remember.
At a young age

you had scarlet fever and were locked away at home.
You told me about cool iron railings of the fence
as you peered through at children going to school,
then back to their warm noisy homes.
Like prison bars they were. Life locked out.
All the company, the fun, scrambling together beyond.

They were scared you were dying.
Grandma nearly died having you.
That makes a mother anxious.
I know. I nearly died in childbirth too.
And your Irish grandfather had buried
five of his brothers and sisters aged one to fourteen,
all dead in four weeks from scarletina,
August 1880, County Limerick.

Do you think your hearing was affected?
My voice was so small to you,
When I opened my lips, it seemed caught
and gusted away, so
I couldn't hear it either.
You had to leave a night-light on
balancing on top of my dusty wardrobe,
or I might have gotten lost in the night.
I might have disappeared.
And no voice to call with.

It was a small lamp – only six inches high.
It had a boiled-egg-white globe
that shone like pearl in hours between dark and light.
I loved it.
Shadow wolves never came near it,
though sometimes I saw you, hovering in the shadows.
These are the farewell days, now.
Leave the light on.
Please.
Leave the light on when you go.

Ausculta

The drawers in my father's house are empty;
you thought his heart was
but it never was.
You couldn't hear him
and maybe he had a different language
those days.
No-one taught him the right words then
or that it was important to use them.
But to you it was, I see that, and
maybe he didn't listen.

Maybe you couldn't hear my brother.
He was small and blond and funny.
He danced for you.
He had a horse on a long green stick,
its name was Trigger.
Do you remember him?
You must remember him.
We loved him so very much.
He made you laugh.
You forgave him everything.

I used to look after him at school.
I was in trouble for that,
hanging around the toilets
to make sure he was ok among the big boys.
The school said you had to stop me,
let him grow up, be independent.
He never forgave me
when I left home at twenty;
nor you when you did later,
at sixty-four.

He stopped being close to you when he was eleven:
'Saw what happened to you,' he says, 'took a step back.'
He wasn't there much at the end.
Maybe he thought you wouldn't notice.
Maybe he was used to that.
He only had to do one thing anyway,
and he was an angel.
One visit made it all ok;
one phone call, one gesture of attention.
One thing from him; never enough from me.

– *Ausculta:* Listen in Latin

Borderlines

There was a door to my wardrobe.
There was even a key. I kept it locked.
Inside, blowsy with love,
there were letters from him –
my first lover at twenty.
Ripe with lust, soaked in outrageous desire
they trembled with erotic tales of his nocturnal dreams
where I flowered,
where I lay in a valley of lilies,
one white arm bent to support my head,
'so lovely I could paint you,' he said,
and much more.

These are private things.

I hid them – they were so intimate – in case:
safe inside the body of my sweater
under a pile of long-sleeved t-shirts,
in a drawer, in a wardrobe, locked;
the key hidden.
That's a long way in to find them.
I bet you smiled when you read them.
I bet you lusted.
You wanted to be me.
You wanted to be inside my skin.
You wanted my life.
You wanted him

because he slept with me, because he loved me.

You never told me until I was thirty-five
at dinner in a restaurant with my new partner, not him.
You told it as a joke.
We were supposed to laugh.
How you had told my father, crushing my rough halo
the day before I turned twenty-one;
how, you had put one over on me –
and later I found, more than one.
Phaedra came close, but even the Greeks failed to cast into myth
all the variations of a mother's possible betrayal.
You giggled, all those years later: naughty, clever schoolgirl.
I remember light glinting off your teeth, mouth saying

'You didn't think there was only one key!'

I was sick. I had to leave disgust in the Ladies',
waves of nausea crashing against the heart,
beating on its old retaining wall.
I drove you home to stay with us in our spare room.
I felt vicious accusing you.
I felt mean and damaging yelling at you –
'It wasn't *your* business
It was *mine*. He was – *mine!*'
'How dare you shut me out!' you screamed.
You didn't understand about doors,
sobbing into the wretched dark
for comfort, for love:

and in the end I gave it.

and the children prosper

I have lived every day with the fear I have damaged them
searching their tears for mine;

their rejections, for the vicious playground I knew,
anxious I might have locked them into our sticky web.

The first came out of your dying, and my own so close,
in birth, my blood a crimson lake across the tiles.

If separation was to threaten death,
with his birth, fact almost made it true.

But I was spared dying to care for him; so he can
bask in sunshine, teach that orb the dazzle of smiling.

The second seemed always freer of me
born with his power beside, not from me.

My fearful clinging kept him ten months inside,
leaping overgrown from the womb.

He draws the moon towards his heart.
She trails after him callow, to learn his craft of shining.

*

I have lived every day with the fear I have damaged them
searching their tears for mine.

I look for my tenderness to them
when I lie down at night.

I look for my listening to them
each day at the end of school.

I watch them roam outside the borders
sharing adventure with friends, returning safe home.

I search them out on a hard day between us,
to say I love them, and I know their love.

*

I have lived every day with the fear I have damaged them.
But awareness can surely alter things to newness.

They rise like golden wheat under a fair sky;
their voices are not shrill but melodious to me.

Their hearts are swollen with the pollen of kindness;
honey rolls from their lips, limbs lithe with strength.

They keep me close but separate.
They tell me not to worry, they do not fear this.

They are full of the grace of those belovéd.
Ringing out across the years: gratitude is my Song of Songs.

If you could have known

If you could have known him now:
a handsome man still, strong and fit
for someone beyond his mid-eighties,
a marvel of clarity and endurance.
Where you thought he never listened,
he does now.
Where you felt invisible,
his vision is always in focus.
Where you thought him cool,
his warmth takes winter from my eyes.

Some of this is due to your passing,
things he learned then about care.

Some of it grew organically;
tentative unfurl of an iris as it opens to early spring,
bulb already preparing for the next.
Some grew with his first grandchildren, my sons:
their smallness, their tender skin against his roughening cheek,
voices sweet, higher than waves,
·pulling him to games of cricket on the beach
calling out to him from along the dunes.
Now they fill into themselves;
tall adolescents, complex, kind, funny.

My brother brings the thrill of difference,
marrying a Turkish-Australian: dark-haired, more than lovely.
Behind her eyes the story of empires,
history of food that spills a long list of names we love to hear,
turning their strangeness along our tongues.
Two more children came late,
out of his worry to get it right:
a boy still small, flinging himself at life his father's way;
a girl-baby with black abundant hair; hazel, curious eyes.
We both left it late, very late, and we've been lucky.

I don't think there was space while you were alive.
You were still trying to loose your tide inside me,
I was busy sandbagging the banks.
I knew strength was limited.
It was survival.
Now, smiles you never knew carry your memory.
We kept all that from you;
that turned out to be true.
No-one denied you on purpose, nothing deliberate;
just the slow movement of death and life renewing itself.

I'm sorry you missed this part: for you, for them.
We just didn't find the key to that locked door in time.

If you could see him now, still fishing the reef,
drinking whiskey with friends, dancing birthdays away,
you wouldn't worry that he's lonely, getting tired.
Older grandchildren want to be near him,
spending holidays at the house
traipsing sand through the hallways, and soon,
taking their small cousins to the shop for ice-cream.
He carries it for you; carries you with him.
You would have loved him still; more.
If you could have known him now.

Out of the labyrinth

We're coming to the end now and I'm holding on.
It seems the string is in *my* hand after all.
Light is opening up ahead, round and warm.

Here is the last kiss; the band is packing up. Grab balloons for the kids;
carry them along with the laughter, the charge,
the blistered gifts.

I remember your irreverence on holidays, striding in shorts and thongs
into fancy hotel dining rooms, dragging us humiliated,
immensely satisfied that you'd broken the rules.

You elbowed your way to the head of so many queues,
saying politely, 'Excuse me, excuse me,'
returning with booty through an astonished throng.

In Paris you did this for tickets to the Folies Begère.
Explaining Dad was deaf, you got front-row seats,
though he spoke no French. 'We had a great view!' you said.

At Shannon airport a sign read, 'Don't park here', and underneath,
'Don't even *think* of parking here'.
You said, 'Forget it. They don't mean us.'

You embarrassed us: wore hot-pink silk pants late in life;
did skits at your local gem club dressed in wig and bikini,
pear-shaped, bottom bouncing, breasts bulging. You loved the stage.

You told lies, and the speed you were doing in that old tank
of a Fairlane actually became twenty kilometres less,
even the cop starting to doubt the corner stop sign.

You had Depression Anxiety, collecting hundreds, no, thousands,
of rubber bands, bits of string, plastic bags, take-away containers,
jelly moulds with holes in them, letters of a lifetime, all those paper kisses.

You had guts. You just wouldn't bow down.
You taught us: 'No is only a word; it can't hurt you.'
But when cancer came, you moved into courage like a skin.

That gathering grace in you, that ordinary heroic,
left a luminous snail-trail for me there in the dark
when cancer struck my breast five years on.

And it drives me, that curiosity you had, ticking in my blood,
taking the boys to feast on wonders in corners of the world:
cathedrals, galleries, ruins, stone fences, a city of canals.

You flooded me, but it taught me the feel inside another's skin;
poetry the only purpose, the one survival.
You didn't know did you? You grew out of the leached soil of your time.

If you sat in the scent-loaded garden beneath windows
in the house on Princess Street and listened, you wouldn't understand me.
You'd still be sad, hurt. And I'd still be sorry.

*

Today my garden is wet with rain, so green in every shade
it could be Eden. But there would be an apple tree, a snake, a choice.
Sun is struggling to light the square of grass outside the open door.

Fruit are coming into this new spring that carries the aching
deadwood from winter, built into what went before, what comes after.
The delicacy of butterflies short-lived is playing with light and shadow.

Sap-filled trunks yield up breath through the lightness of leaves,
shades draining away, brushing trees, rustling their joyful departure
from the heaviness of soil. You want to go with them. I know.

Finally then.
Remember, in spite of scars, it never did fail,
love.

III

By way of light

Portrait
for Raffaella

Lap full of sun torched through the skylight
in this house moving in and out of the heat,
I am told to sit silent where everything moves
except the face straining not to express.
Some think truth is revealed in movement around a mouth.

Deep cello plays with the scent of oriental lilies
pulling it back and forth on a loom of music –
through the dust-flecks dancing,
through the rough scratch of brush on canvas –
in this moment everything ravelled.

Thoughts ripple in the strings' trawled wake:
I stare at your gallery of faces; at the long path behind me;
at my saffron-coloured fingers the lily stamens pushed against
this morning, their pollen tips staining like memory, like love,
blushing for the secret pink of women's dreams.

Blue is your colour, and mine;
it is strung around your hips in a tattoo
twisted from the Irish *Book of Kells*;
it draws my profile across the stretched frame;
it fills my eye cobalt-dark.

Between skin and brush there is no mask,
no brilliant disguise allowed
in the empty space between self, and the idea of self.
They will say you never captured my fire.
But that's what can be seen.

You painted the other side of smiling:
those inner wasted plains; that lost despair;
sadness; and the draughty absence of light
I always called home. Preparing to leave this place,
shocked – I see the past in a frame, snap-frozen.

Deliver us

Egyptian mummies with their bandaged art
slumber golden in Melbourne Museum.
Vermeer's suspended love letter and long-ago life
brocade the ordinary in antique frames in the Gallery.
Haunting vignettes of the fading life of oyster farmers
linger from the cinema trailing brackish memory.

This city is so still and black, leaving a day full of art and history,
driving through sleeping streets out along the revolving earth.
Stars blink their observations from the depth of space, and roads
shimmer under a varnish of light rain,
the moon's long sigh of contentment
an amber sash of highway in the broad dark.

Yet round the next curve of horizon
ridged scarlet with dawn's bright sea,
one red double-decker bus is blowing apart.
Underground, in a maze of tracks, the Minotaur's offspring
bellow for sacrifice, monstrous and cowardly,
their ignorance exploding to pierce the early day.

Everything we know animal in ourselves is there.
Madrid, Casablanca, Riyadh, Baghdad – London:
fear that wedges a cornered child, an adult,
onto the sticky blood-dark seat of a train carriage;
the vicious grip that presses, from a distance,
the phone, the button, the command tool

guiding the indiscriminate impulse
that hits 'soft' targets
full of the everyday business of life;
the mind that orders random, deliberate death,
making mockery of the hurried good-byes at breakfast
no-one imagined really were.

Everything we know of ourselves is there.
Madrid, Casablanca, Riyadh, Baghdad – London.
A man helps a woman's terrified fingers hold on her burnt face,
lifting her stunned, open-eyed towards the light;
passers-by tenderly wrap silver blankets round the shredded clothes,
the naked shock, the missing limbs of strangers.

Into this day, spears of gladioli
strike golden in London parks.
The painter lifts his brush to capture the slanted steamy light
of summer love on a boy's cheek;
a girl raises her viola towards the pulse at her neck,
its strings deep and mellow over the wood's cavernous heart.

A stranger's comfort cups the shoulder of a traveller
shivering in shock.
Kindness and beauty struggle to recall
everything fine and lovely the human hand can do;
and in the deep white wards,
the quiet stitching of a wounded faith.

Ringing you on
i.m. Shelton Lea, poet, 1946-2005

The earth is still ringing
they tell us Shelley,
from the great quake
that split plates of rock,
hammering her frame,
shocking the sea to blue heights
forced to rush headlong in a death scythe
that cut ten countries short.
Five months later,
sea gypsies are tentatively testing their element,
ready to trust again in the sanctity of tides,
to believe in the ongoing gift of things natural,
death and rebirth.

Breath a struggling reverb in your bell-tower of ribs
you slipped away into silence
this summery May, a Friday 13th
full of the glory of omens
that the old ways tell us mean nothing sinister:
Freya's day, goddess of love and sacred poems,
of moon and sea, and the underworld.
Five days later, I remember when we first met,
flowers flourishing rose and lavender at Heidi,
you, carrying in the tray with orange cake and tea,
while Barrett and I sat working over poems.
We lounged, the three of us, talking, talking.
You told stories of pavements and concrete walls,
prejudice, prison bars, and hard immovable things.

You and I:
we always kept Barrett with us after he died.
I think of you both now
as I stand in my dark garden

hung with wet moon-drops,
rain coming at last into our powdery drought.
Full moon is lingering,
its circlet of moon-bow
an oil-slick of iris-blue, purple and green.
The shower has left autumnal flame-flickers
laminate in the trees, to be licked
and polished ruby by dawn's sun.
You waited too long to visit.

I have a photo: our last reading at La Mama.
Profile half-shadowed,
your face is flushed with poetry, with farewell.
Leaving for six weeks away, I didn't know to say good-bye.
If I had, what would I have said?
When friends die, Shelley, there is a quietness left behind
as if the world had always been flat after all,
and they had simply stepped off.
It lasts our lifetime, this silent shape,
its form at first taking the body's space,
then the outline of voice;
finally, the essence of presence, the unshapeable,
stories of the heart that etch in grief.

In Karlovassi, Samos, where I lived a moment
while your days were shortening,
bells from Greek Orthodox churches
carillon each other across the valley of terracotta roofs
toward olive groves on Mt Kerki; towards the unspeakable blue.
They play rhythms you can dance to,
tonal melodies you can hum,
bell-ringers enraptured, with their roughened hands, their joy.
There must be a pattern, a timetable they ring in,
a campanology of intimate meaning,
but to me they came suddenly each time, surprising, unexpected.
And after the bells, cadences remain, hanging in the orange trees
a threaded mesh of chimes and sweet white scent.

No-one tolled those bells for you, Shelley.
No-one stopped the clocks
or draped the panes in black.
These useful rituals of pause, of notification, are lost now.
When you died, the day was startled,
ocean stunned quiet
in my backyard flowering with pink impatiens.
There was the slow, mute, dropping of leaves.
I watched. Then, I could feel it everywhere,
trembling resonant
in shock, loss, maybe some kind of ecstasy:
the whole earth still ringing;
ringing for you, Shelley – ringing you on.

Trawling

You inhabit your skin
fully,
live it from the core
right up to the surface,
where solidity of matter
vanishes into air.
I know how to call you now –
what shape for my parted lips,
were to beat my tongue
on the tang of nipple,
what sweet song you come for.

You have slipped
beneath my wary eyes,
shadow of your head along my breast,
nerves of your fingertips
phosphorescent on my arms
tingling in the dark
beside your noisy sleep.
Your mouth trawling
left a moonlight lattice of salt crystal
trailing inside my thighs.

Your webbed hands
swam into me,
the inland sea I'd long forgotten
flooding again wild with life
as if long years of drought
had been a storage of desire,
not an absence.
But these are virtues of flesh only.

The heart inhabits another place.
Long ago I replaced its blood
with deep-sea water;
its plum-purple chambers
will not get too hot,
chilled
to the breath of winter.

Meeting when we're almost young
you might convince me of hope.
That is the off-beat thud
of its small pinioned wing I hear
against the ribs of domesticity.
You tell me I need to fall in love,
and your plane takes off
unsubtle in its stiffened silver plumage.
The owl tattooed on your right shoulder blade
spreads its unserrated wings for you,
its silent flight cutting the yellow buttery dawn.
These are the leaving hours.

There, in skies of flesh and blue
there are things
that do not speak of brokenness.
Here, on the ground,
where breath is held, waiting,
you have slid between nerves and bone
almost to the heart's barred cage.

Harvesting

Wind on my belly this uncertain summer,
I garden half-naked, free of children;
without you,
a castaway in Eden.
This ladder is high for apricots.
Risking balance, stretching to gather all I can,
I think of you that humid weekend
rocking on the prow of the boat laughing, rod heavy with squid.
'God of the fishes', I called you, sarong painted with them
swimming wildly in circles round your haunches.

Only four bags of fruit
when last year there were thirty.
Blossom left the bough too fast.
I remember it – all in one night –
while you slept and I lay wide-eyed, hopeful,
in that hotel with white bathrobes.
Next day the lawn was powdered white and pink
with apricot and cherry plum snow.
It was windy and a cool
unpredictable spring.

Breasts swaying cockeyed, scarred among ripening figs
I'm tidying lower branches
that might decay.
I know that in summer's heat, if it comes,
I'll open their flesh hot from the tree
tongue their fuschia-pink filaments
and gorge as if lonely.
I think of your lips burgundy with cherry juice
my hands mottled-red, feeding them to you
driving to the bay in a pirate's fog.

Between my thighs, passionfruit vine shivers a thrill,
yet it has more than enough
to entwine itself with: the fence,
the creeping mexican blood flower,
open red throats rioting.
Fruit hang bulbous,
still green and full of promises
after the passion flowers:
their starry yellow eyes,
their purple feather mouths.

Bees are jealous of their lavender.
They try to follow me into the house,
stalks and flowers crushed into my hands.
They don't understand
about clearing out old undergrowth,
pruning for greater abundance.
They do understand though
about harvesting pollen like memories,
about storage
and the transformation of small things into sweetness.

Small miracle

Seven thousand four hundred bike riders
that weighed down two ferries crossing the Tasman,
churn down the Brooker Highway into Hobart
decked out for Christmas,
antlers on top of helmets,
tinsel trailing spun-sunshine in a toffee-hot day.
Skulls and crossbones shrouded in Santa red,
white beards are a fluttering wake, wave after wave.

Rushing to KMart for a last minute present
we are stopped by police holding back the
domestic tide of respectable shoppers,
an eager fringe of onlookers keenly waving.
Bikers with pillion soft-toys, or
giant pandas and teddies
bouncing berserk on their handlebars,
roar towards the Children's Hospital.

First in line at the traffic lights, we idle excited.
I wave until both arms ache, grinning,
a child in me I thought had never been there
stretching forward to be chosen for attention,
straining to connect, to catch the glance of eyes,
from these Darth Vaders dressed as elves.
They raise their green wands toward me,
delight a sugary ache, tasting of donut-cinnamon.

Cabaret skids from the radio. I hear its harmony.
One arm resting across the back of the car seat
I cup your shoulder blade, its tattooed owl stunned beneath,
wings shuddering eager for flight;
or is it your voice that vibrates,
resonating in the inner palm of my hand
as you read me Paul Muldoon's poems
with their earthed, peaty mouths?

Evasive all my life: the ripe shape, the feel of happiness.
Struck mute, I want to tell you.
I turn to you: lakes of your blue eyes deepening
as mine flood, pouring tenderly across a dry land.
I want to tell you, but words make it too small.
They promised this. They said, when the Dark starts moving,
slipping in wider and wider the light –
the light, the whole big sky of light, begins to open like a crack.

Three on a boat

Sea mist breathes out along Pirate's Bay.
In the space where the rocky headland cracks open
dark-throated caves are holding all sunlight hostage.
Gulls ramble in their cries; their wings
slice gauzy sky clean as a filleting knife.
There are sheds of grey timber and corrugated tin
near the trees before sand runs down to the shore's edge.
The dog's barking in circles and you're weighing stones carefully
like you have to get to know them first,
and then you stand up and swing back your arm.

Mesmeric it is from across the water:
the bend, collection, ready shoulder, strong pitch.
I can see you at seventeen, a too-fast bowler that had to be slowed
and no-one noticing what that meant,
when you needed noticing.
And they skim, these stones –
once, twice, anything up to thirty skips
and you yell at me across the water
where I sit doubtful on the jetty, legs dangling like a kid:
'Here it comes – right to ya, Ben.'

I laugh because 'it is too far so,'
but sure – there it comes, there it comes –
warmth of your palm-print still cupping it,
jumping, leaping, and then,
the slishing slide.
Spouting tiny bubbles,
it falls through shallow water
to the slope of mottled sand beneath my feet.
'You're a genius!' I yell, and I mean it.

Waiting for Rick to bring the boat now, we're both on the jetty
our shadow-feet dancing together then apart on ripples,
and in that shade a wobbygong is snapping a fish frame.
The shark turns in a death roll like a croc,
fish spine in its mouth undulating.
We watch the simple swathe of it, draped and swirling,
a Chinese gymnast's flag furling and unfurling,
over-energetic next to our laziness, our Sunday disorder.
We've forgotten so much:
sweaters, my lunch, deep-sea rods.

You two settle for the boat to be off-shore,
too much veiled damp to risk open sea.
You did this right, you and he,
along the line of years since you were sixteen.
If you're lucky, that tangles itself together
in a knot that holds through all weathers.
You stand on the boat's prow and your body angles content:
light rod, broad hat, sarong of fishes
that will hopefully call up the real thing.
I loll against the seat, languid on Kwells, Rick up back opening beer.
Banter is on fishing: memories of fish, today's fish, fish to come.

I know this language of the boat; the ease of it; closeness.
Your hands tying knots of patience around the hook
are my father's hands, my grandfather's,
and you bringing me something of them:
straight like them, a little round at the middle, hair greying to trust,
squint of blue eyes against the sun's reflection.
Here there are no secrets between us and the sea;
no spaces left for misunderstanding.
This is really simple, friendship. And this stays with me.
It's the open child, it's pure song:
three on a boat that's not pea-green.

Couta are cutting lines, but suddenly – squid –
dancing across the water on the hook
fluttering their wings like a flying manta ray I saw off Heron
stunned at its flight through air.
I thrust the net down, watch their rage,
a black hole in blue water.
'Do it quick,' I say,
your knife bringing on a fringe of neon-green pulse
before death shocks it marble-white.

On landing I hold the squid,
candles dangling slick-sticky across my arm.
Your hands black with ink, write their eulogy with
knife-sharp calligraphy in the sand.
Slicing them, turning bodies inside out, you clean their pearly flesh
ready to swim in lime and ginger back at Rick's,
you cooking while I mix mango salad,
our tongues tingling with anticipation and chilli,
scent of mint in our skin, crushed on our smiling lips.
Then, wine, for such a day of stumbling perfection,
for love of friendship,
for our song of the squid hunt,
for everything that comes with the memory of
three on a boat, sharing it.

Govetts Leap, Blackheath, Blue Mountains

for Mari and Suzanne

Mountains here shudder with reverb,
hit repeatedly with bolts of lightning.
Water and crumbling tremors are shape-shifters for an earth
too old to be bothered changing; that steals blue from the sky,
blue from the secret orchids shaping their flowers for sunlight.
The closer you get, the further it recedes,
that haze of violets travelling after a trail of rainbows.
Earth here is tanned and broken, falling into the lap of rock.
Not a country for centaurs or fairies,
the shades here are brown and live inside ochre
and the old stone-people stories.

Among red-faced cliffs embarrassed at their naked skin,
beside Govetts Hanging Gardens at the Leap,
falls parachute thousands of metres in their glide,
constantly renew the wet needs of vegetation as it swings
in heavy curtains of weeping green.
Insect-eating plants insinuate their thin wrists in seduction,
minute hairs upright; sticky, the lick of death.
Bladderworts sift their microscopic food from droplets.
Sundews trap those flying blind,
while their flowers, innocently clean,
allow the miracle of pollination.

Valleys carouse to and fro between talons of rock,
as if a giant river had rushed its way forward to the long, long away sea.
Orange lichen flame across boulders.
Touching it could make a hand-print brilliant in the dark of caves.
Warratahs clot crimson in the bush, their bracts bent back
each petal bulbous with one unspent trembling tear.
Water thrusts itself over the scarp, plummeting, diving,
arrowheads white and spinning
striking accurate the crests of protruding ledge
whitening it to instant snow,
then vapourous in wind-lift; rising, rising

Unlocking

Wentworth Falls, above Valley of the Waters, with Suzanne

Peaks have strut across valleys in front of me,
gorges loosened their raiment of dull green,
falling agape, exposing sandstone skin powdered turmeric.
Bush has yielded up strips of native orchid,
beetroot-bright lips trembling,
yet I remain unopened, unmoved – a simple lockout.
Trudging the crumble of cliff-edges listening for echoes,
I've glanced down pathways hoping to burrow into this place,
into these mountains by whose sorcery
those around me are bound with wonder.
Feeling landlocked still,
I am grief-heavy, disconnected.

Now, this Weeping Rock, its lament whimpering from a distance,
its showers treble-high at first, thudding deeper the closer we come
until birds are drowned in it. A mountain's tears gush a melody
so wrought I think of cellos, their long strings of melancholy.
Crossing stepping-stones at its pool's edge, we lean over:
layer on layer, a sigh of veil falling towards a lost valley below.

Tombstones of slab cut from the crags' soft haunch with picks
lead down, down, in vertical decline,
then out, lost in vacant sky.
You have no anxiety in the descent,
making my fear more serious, more surmountable.
Superstition is a spine in shiver.
I fear spirits of stone and wind: we have no bargain.
Terror shakes me with the wind rising.
It shudders the railing to unpeal my grip.
Then, almost a trip as the wind drops suddenly, edge a slip away.

Lower we go, where a deep pool languishes at mid-level drop,
water plunging a thousand metres yet into a valley lake,

so far below, the stream's final plash is truant.
Arms open, wild with heights, you talk of flying, as if below
those mouth-blown heads of gums are sponge and moss,
or some springy bog that will give you succour, a soft landing.

Resting, we ooze bare feet into soft mud under cool showers.
Above us, a worn spur is basking rusted-amber in late day,
small globes of its cascade, sun-polished forties ticker-tape,
flickering, bursting to spray all over us.
Licking skin, tinselling hair, water is a lover experimenting with touch.
Languid, we watch sun fragmenting spindrift
into a parted lip of rainbow.
The tramp up is, as it should be, easier; ascension steep but unmisted.
'One moment, one step; one step, one moment,'
you remind me calmly, exhausted with exclamation.

Halfway back you call to me to try for echoes.
Unleashed, it screams from me, harsh, animal, unshaped by word,
full of an ancient grief gutted of dialect. So *this* is a screaming place.
'Funny, I can hear the echo only where you are, not up here,' you cry.
At the top pool, leaning over the rail, it frizzes over us in our delight:
water falling upwards, a final spray of silver in late light.

Behind closed lids sleeping that night,
only the scattered sheen of that last effervescence lingers.
Falls, rock, heights, have cast me empty;
swept out, washed clean, the cave of the mouth before sound;
knowing myself small in this, diminished,
and, strangely, by that smallness reassured.
Waking, eyes will be salt-ringed; body weightless, supple,
unscarred and free of burdens, almost holy;
as if, outside language, beyond the body,
through opened pores of earth, air, water;
there is a lightness of vapour
to which we can and will, return.

Things you gave me

for Susan Gallagher, 2004

It begins russet-henna at the centre
moving out through electric orange – flaming montbretia
or sunset over Connemara shores.
It keeps darkening to burgundy heather,
and the purple-brown of bog hills in winter.
Long and wide this chiffon scarf you gave me
though not as long
as the distance I travel from you.

Strange that the colours are the same as those rugs
I bought from Máire Ní Thaidhg,
hand-woven from earth to flame,
warm across my bed, skeined with fine threads of sky-blue
and a slit of green sea that splits the rocks in Mannin Bay.
I sleep each night under the crust of that land,
under that sun going to its rest,
though broad is the ocean between us.

Light as a hot day's gingery haze, that scarf.
You must have been thinking of summer
in your whitewashed cottage
with its heretical yellow windows,
though this year I came out of season,
trees shocked and leafless,
winter's dark meniscus of burnt almond
skin-tight over the land.

Too early for golden blooms, green spears of bog-iris
thrust up through the turf, fields of them gathering
to shame the armies outside the walls of Troy.
But cherry trees further south were blossom-loaded,
gyrating wildly in the wind to drop their pink pom-poms
across pavements, crowded into gutters,

catching in our hair and our laughing mouths
racing to escape the rain.

I spared nothing this time with the peat,
banked it up high, fierce lava-beds thick in the grate.
Finally learning the skill of raking a fire, each day I relit it
from coals I'd hidden under ash the night before.
I love best that phoenix flame.
I'd stand in the dark outside
just to hear the sea break stones on Drimeen and
taste comfort in the cindery air.

I didn't mind the cold.
Even sleet couldn't chill the glow off returning.
Friends called my borrowed house a *shebeen*.
Too much wine we had,
to feed my gluttony for their company,
for music, for words,
for the stroke of Ireland on my skin, and deeper,
a spun-thread to carry back in my veins.

Leaving, you gave me a Claddagh ring
fearful that my own small version, not gifted by a friend,
is tarnished by that lack. You knew then, and you know now,
friendship is threaded in this warp of coming and going,
across the weft of things left and taken:
fabric on skin, colour-infused memory,
the land, the flame, the dance of the cherry trees.
And this ring, my silver currency of remigration.
I never take it off.

— *shebeen*: inn or whiskey house
— *Claddagh:* an old Irish ring depicting the heart for love, held in the hands
for friendship and crowned for loyalty.

All changing things

for Lynda Burke, April 2004

Striding the track before I leave, wind blows strong
from the west towards you, far east in Dublin city.
Clean off the Atlantic, it brings you Errislannan's
white luminance; night's shawl of lost light
that drifts from the hollow wings of angels.

Bluebells, the violet eyes of spring, are its guide.
It shivers through the gilded glitter shaken from Mebh's laugh,
golden fleece of gorse and primrose that threaded,
weaves your name among those on the list
for whom candles burn; for comfort, for healing.

I see it blowing back your long sun-stroked hair,
carrying an Egyptian vial in which tears are saved for mourning.
Your mother is gravely ill, changing from herself into the other,
the one who leans on you,
who gathers her past and casts it toward the darkening earth.

On Monday you watched her eyes leave her, momentarily,
before the fall, the stopped heart;
before your frantic prayers caught the winging soul.
Hospital-white now, her breath a machine-blown kiss,
her food is a belly of tubes.

Her lids are closed, leaving the room tidy of sight.
You hover with her; with decisions that come too soon.
Speak to her, I urge; wade in toward her through the fog of coma,
tell her how you long to hear her voice
even if the telling is to hear your own.

Fear rattles in your throat.
But this may not be death.
Perhaps she comes into the next stage of living,
and you are about to learn the tongue of middle-life
that carries both voice and memory for the old.

I think of my own mother dead these fourteen years.
I wonder is your own like her, unable to hear;
locked into the inner wasteland of despair,
forever calling to be saved, to be loved; not understanding,
a mother's task is to care for; a child's to grow away.

Shafts of bog-iris are plentiful this year,
sharp at the road's edge, their yellow shining
a sheathed promise I will not see, weeks from now.
Flung across the bog, they seem to lack design,
scattering like unmatched spokes from a thousand broken wheels.

A dead pilot whale is wedged
between rocks at Ceánn Doolin,
great tail stilled, eyes on inward journeys,
spout's wet breath scattered among rainbows
way out beyond the false terminus of horizon.

Its pink blubber is weeping oil,
rid of skin that greyly set itself as barrier
between every fleshy sense, and the air's chiffon touch.
Perhaps nothing really divides, dies, or falls beyond transformation, and
everything on this last walk is change only, or renewal.

– *Mebh*: Maeve, Goddess of Connaught

There is an answer: Who are you?
for Subhana Barzaghi Roshi, Vipassana retreat, Hawkesbury

I   I am tears
     I am suffering
     I am beyond that
     I am the stretched blue
     I am above; above-ness
     I am silence, stillness
     I am Breath
     I am the caught breath
     I am nothing

     I don't want to leave, move.
     No feeling, no thought – suspended.
     You stand behind me.
     I hear your presence

     but no-one comes.
     Where is the breath? – arrested –
     held here in a home-ness
     fully unfamiliar.

     Your voice calls me back.
     There's the risk – choosing it –
     the non-returning,
     the stopped breath.

II   The mind comes with words.
     The mind comes with names
       that do not fit.
     There is no signpost, no gate nor fence.

     The mind comes with fear.
     It might be lost here
     if there are no names.
     But there is no need for a word.

     The mind comes with a sly smile:
       it was imagined only.

But no, there was no volition,
imagining being an act of will.

Now mind comes with memory
to fetch it back.
But it is not in memory;
how can it be?

It is not a pasture of mind,
not a place to revisit.
It is beyond;
it is between the dark and the light.

Now comes the trying,
to force the way back,
uncover entrance.
Now comes longing

to return there, to get back,
but there are myriad pathways
covered in brambles of the mind;
labyrinths, mazes, trickster mirrors.

One has the light of joy,
another, the pain of suffering:
all false entrance.
Only one way – unknowing.

Now I see why there are riddles,
words jumbling to dis-explain,
to expose that which is only clear
in the caught breath.

Now I know the meaning of the bell
tolling across the gateway,
across the sill between worlds,
fetching us back, until it is time

for the last breath.

Beyond white

for Susan Gallagher, March 2006.

*

They have rolled you round on their treadmill wheel.
They have taken from you: blood, time.
Your body defeats them,
keeps clocking in unyellowed though tired,
spirit cleaning away a liver so full of tumour
it shames the bulbous baobab tree.

That tree, envious of flower and fruit,
gods uprooted and struck into the earth
so it lives as if upside down
its branches confused capillary roots
dangling for sustenance in the sky.
Everything is like that now.

I no longer know what view to take, what is real,
whether we fly clear-eyed towards the horizon
or wrong way up, night-blind,
speed disoriented toward the edge of earth
they said was not there,
grappling frantic for knowledge in the pale air.

Doctors prance through spinning turnstiles
to this merry-go-round, horses with their painted faces;
impossible to tell which is magician or trickster god; which the sage.
One speaks of death, another acceptance;
our last good knight promises life shining along his knife.
I weigh them, scales haphazard as I strive to sew you to us.

There are things I do not fear for you.
I have seen you translucent, hair spun-sapphire
under light I thought from a lamp.
I held you close, luminous blue, for you to whisper,
'I love you. I'm glad you've come.'
I entered the circle for you; and the faery cleft.

There are things I do not fear for you.

*

Soon, the window I gaze through will not be your lens of home
in which you watch the ocean
crusted cream on tar-black rocks,
body breaking open to heal itself each day in its salt,
ready to again unstitch its wounds for us; its ivory scars.
I'm searching for a way to bind you tight to this sea, this land.

When I'm replaced across exiling waters,
voice a disembodied thread in a mystery of connection,
each day in your struggle of waiting
hold onto one lovely thing – saying to me when I call:
'This is it,' – and tell me,
as I tell you, this March morning on Errislannan:

*

I know silence is the bog;
that is earth's gift to us when we learn to lose our own babble.
I love the way sound sinks in; disappears into wet earth,
its mouth taking a reversal of language into its heart, its broken lung,
tongue stilled, voice unnecessary cargo.
But now I know an even greater quiet.

Today dawn was silent snow; silent beyond white, beyond silence.
Its breath had scattered flurries
across the barbed-wire fence iced crystal-green,
cows standing shocked-black
on bogland unused to it, whiter than salt,
all the way to the stones and the dark, dark sea.

Éiru's bare shoulder was cloaked under it,
each cheek of bog a frosted wish,
hollowed elbows of rock brimful, dazzling bright
where thumb of night had pushed it in.
Powder finer than breath, collecting in frozen fragments,
it spiralled to pack hard, Lynda's house bejewelled,
sun cutting diamonds across the terrace.

Full moon had shaken herself over the land.
I saw her in the night, generous,
cobalt veins opening into midnight's sky, and the bay's lap.
The limen between her gardenia glaze and snow and
bleached hope, indiscernible;
nothing but imagined barriers, clever horizons of the mind,
when all around we know this alabaster loveliness.

These things settle the heart,
make doubt and knowledge,
sweetness and sorrow, the same.
Soul flows infinite, without a rent.
Leaving, I remain.
Behind us is, as it is; before us, as it will be,
and on the hill, a swinging gate.